W9-BDY-088

Jerome A. Chanes

HEBREWSPEAK

HEBREWSPEAK

An Insider's Guide
to the Way Jews Think

Joseph Lowin

JASON ARONSON INC.
Northvale, New Jersey
London

This book was set in 11 pt. Baskerville
by Kelby and Teresa Bowers, Compublishing of Cincinnati, Ohio.

Copyright © 1995 Joseph Lowin

10   9   8   7   6   5   4   3   2   1

All rights reserved. Printed in the United States of America. No part of this book may be used or reproduced in any manner whatsoever without written permission from Jason Aronson Inc. except in the case of brief quotations in reviews for inclusion in a magazine, newpaper, or broadcast.

Library of Congress Cataloging-in-Publication Data

Lowin, Joseph.
    Hebrewspeak : an insider's guide to the way Jews think / by Joseph
Lowin.
        p.   cm.
    Includes bibliographical references.
    ISBN 1–56821–418–9
    1. Hebrew language – Social aspects. 2. Jews – Attitudes.
    3. Hebrew language – Terms and phrases. 4. Hebrew language – Roots.
    5. Judaism – Terminology. 6. Hebrew language – Religious aspects –
    Judaism. I. Title.
    PJ 4544.75.L68   1995
    492.4'8 – dc20   94-46454

Manufactured in the United States of America. Jason Aronson Inc. offers books and cassettes. For information and catalog write to Jason Aronson Inc., 230 Livingston Street, Northvale, New Jersey 07647.

To the memory of my father,

ABRAHAM LOWIN

אַבְרָהָם בֶּן יִשְׂרָאֵל צְבִי

who taught me to take Hebrew words seriously

by playing with them.

And to the memory of my father-in-law,

ABRAHAM WADLER

אַבְרָהָם אַרְיֵה בֶּן יוֹסֵף

who taught how to combine self-respect and dignity

with good humor.

אַתָּה הוּא

אֲשֶׁר בָּחַרְתָּ בְּאַבְרָם וְהוֹצֵאתוֹ מֵאוּר כַּשְׂדִּים,

וְשַׂמְתָּ שְׁמוֹ אַבְרָהָם: וּמָצָאתָ אֶת לְבָבוֹ נֶאֱמָן

לְפָנֶיךָ

עִבְרִית הִיא שְׂפַת עַמֵּנוּ וְּדַבֵּר בָּה

Contents

CONTENTS

CONTENTS

CONTENTS   xi

CONTENTS

CONTENTS   XV

Acknowledgments

Some ten years ago, a meeting was held in the office of Alan Tigay, executive editor of *Hadassah Magazine*, about the future of the Hebrew column, a regular feature of the magazine for many years. All agreed that its readership was very limited. Only one person, elitist in the extreme – myself, as it happened – was pleased with the way things were, a column entirely in Hebrew available only to a happy few. Since there were very few readers to whom the column was accessible, one faction, interested in the maximal use of editorial space, wished to do away with it entirely; for the others it was a matter of Zionist ideology: *Hadassah Magazine* without Hebrew was unthinkable. They suggested the column be overhauled completely, by finding an author who could write interestingly about Hebrew in English. Ideology won and the meeting ended with the editor committed to finding an author.

As we were filing out of the office, the editor turned to me and asked me to stay behind. Would I like to try my hand at inventing a new type of Hebrew column? "Why me?" I asked. After all, writing a Hebrew column was the furthest thing from my mind at the time. His answer was enigmatic, ambiguous, almost mystical: "Because I trust you." To this day, I don't know whether he trusted me to be accurate or interesting or funny, or whether he trusted me to maintain the level of journalistic professionalism to which he had committed the magazine, or whether he just trusted me not to make a fool of myself. What I do know is that for the past ten years I have labored to earn his trust. It gives me great pleasure to acknowledge here that thanks to Alan Tigay's trust – whatever that meant to him – a new outlet for my creativity opened to me, one that began with a Hebrew column, then led to a stint on *Kol Yisrael*, Israel's radio network, doing a segment called "Hebrew Roots & Sources," and finally turned into this book.

I would also like to thank the other people at *Hadassah Magazine*, my editors, Roselyn Bell Baskin and Zelda Shluker, and their assistants, for making sure that what I had written was both accurate and interesting. I owe a great debt of gratitude as well to the many readers of the column who have taken the time and trouble to write me or to come up to me in person with suggestions about the ways some of the things that I had written might be enhanced and extended. Many of their suggestions have found their way into the newly revised chapters of the present book. I trust that they will recognize their contributions. A special vote of thanks to the editorial staff at Jason Aronson Inc., especially Janet Warner and Muriel Jorgensen, who made a difficult editing and proofreading task seem routine.

The period of my life that had the most influence on the development of my Hebrew language skills and on my very attachment to the Hebrew language were the years I spent at Massad, a Hebrew-language camp whose "graduates," now living in both Israel and America, were the people I imagined I was "Hebrewspeaking" with as I wrote these pieces. Not only are they — in their unconditional love of Hebrew, Israel, and Jews — the ideal audience for this work, they are also among its collaborators.

I am often asked how I choose the words about which I write. One of my greatest pleasures — as it was my late father's, may his memory be for a blessing — is to listen to the words of the Torah reading in the synagogue on *Shabbat* morning. As I listen and follow along in my *humash*, a strange word, or a strange usage of a familiar word, will strike my ear. From that moment, I am as if possessed. The word resonates in my head during the rest of the service and on the walk home.

At the *Shabbat* table, after *kiddush*, I share with my family my excitement at making this new discovery. All of a sudden, the table is covered with dictionaries of biblical, rabbinic, modern, and slang Hebrew, and with concordances and commentaries. I tell myself that all this is done purely for the sake of learning, with no practical intention of using this knowledge for any other purpose, however lofty. Nevertheless, I will soon blurt out to my family, "What do you think? Wouldn't this word make for a good column?" Almost inevitably, in the ten years that I have been writing the column, one of my children — Shari, David, or Benjamin — who grew up with an obsessive father and therefore learned to be laconic, will say, "You know, Dad, I came across another word this week in school. You might want to think of using it." Deflated and elated at the same time, I now have two words to muse about. Almost without fail, it is the children's suggestion that makes its way into the column. The column is then sent off. But not before my wife, Judy, has had her go at it, making sure that the finished product is free of pedantry, esotericism, and just plain buffoonery. It is to Judy above all that readers of this book owe its readability, as it is to her that I owe everything else.

Introduction

"Hebrew is not a language; Hebrew is magic." I am told this, not by some wild-eyed mystical kabbalist encountered in the Negev desert or in the hills of the Galilee but on the streets of Tel Aviv, by a plain Jew, a middle-class urban Israeli, a rationalist if ever there was one.

He goes on to explain that for him Hebrew is magic, not because it contains some hidden secrets about the meaning of the universe but because if you stare at a Hebrew word long enough, it will reveal its own meanings to you. "Hebrew is magic," he tells me, "because, like the beloved in the Song of Songs, it opens itself up to you. With its nouns and its verbs, its adjectives and its adverbs, its actives and its passives, all referring back to a three-lettered root, it invites and encourages you to come into the center of its essence.

"Of course, that is no small thing," he continues. "Hebrew is magic because, in opening up for you a pathway to understanding words, it teaches you to understand the history and the values of the people who use them, the Jews. It is the insider's guide to the way Jews think. As such, it also teaches you to understand yourself as a Jew."

I myself do not know much about magic, but I do know something about pleasure. And this much I can say: there is much pleasure to be derived — exquisite pleasure, the pleasure usually associated with romantic love — from looking at, and into, Hebrew words.

As the Hebrew columnist for *Hadassah Magazine*, I have been looking into Hebrew words systematically for more than ten years. I can report that sometimes this pleasure translates itself into something more than mere pleasure. Sometimes, if you do it right, this activity leads to moments of sheer happiness, moments that one would not like to see come to an end.

Of what does this pleasure, this happiness, consist? I am willing to accept my interlocutor's analysis. It consists of nothing more or less than the discovery that one can gain understanding, through one's language, of one's people and of one's self, that by getting inside the Hebrew language one can trace the thought processes of the Jews.

In reworking the columns for this book, many of which were written to coincide with a theme of the issue in which they appeared, often a Jewish holiday, I discovered that with some rewriting they would lend themselves admirably to an alphabetical presentation, forming something like a dictionary of basic Jewish concepts. This is the form adopted here. Even the last eight chapters, which do not deal strictly with roots and are therefore found after the alphabetical listings, are about Jewish concepts and try to offer insights into the ways Jews think.

A word about transliteration – the translation of the Hebrew alphabet into the Roman – is in order. For the most part I have followed the general transliteration rules found on page 90 and the spelling of the letters of the Hebrew alphabet found on page 304 of volume 1 of the *Encyclopaedia Judaica* (Jerusalem: Keter Publishing House, 1972). Although I have tried to remain consistent in my transliterations, I have not permitted concern for consistency to get in the way of the reader's comfort. The reader will easily get used to the following: (1) when the *letters* of the Hebrew alphabet are "romanized," they are presented in uppercase roman type; (2) all Hebrew words are followed by a transliteration in parentheses in italics, more or less according to the general system of the *Encyclopaedia Judaica*; (3) Hebrew words – and especially names – given only in English are presented the way they are most commonly spelled, except in the rare cases where I let my petulance about "correct spelling" get in the way.

One more clarification is in order. During the course of this book, I will often write that a word is derived from a three-letter consonantal root, as though at one time people spoke in roots or thought of roots as they spoke. While this is obviously not the way things happened, it is nevertheless a convenient way to write and think of the formation of Hebrew words. As Uzzi Orni of the Hebrew University writes in his article, "Hebrew Grammar," in the *Encyclopaedia Judaica* (8:104), "Clearly, the Hebrew root is only the abstract basis of a family of words used in the language, and does not denote the origin from which the words are derived, as it is hard to assume any level of the language in which the speaker was able to pronounce consonants alone as words. However, the fact that it is an abstraction is not to say that it is a grammatical fiction and merely a technical tool for the analysis of linguistic forms; it is in fact a living reality, an integral part of the structure of the language, which every Hebrew speaker feels."

The way Hebrew speakers feel – and think – is the subject of the pages that follow.

I

אֹזֶן

ALEF, ZAYIN, NUN

ALL EARS

When Marie Antoinette said "Let them eat cake," she committed a fatal error: she didn't attribute enough importance to the bakers of her realm. Jews don't make such mistakes. They honor their bakers' contributions because they know that without bakers they wouldn't be able to celebrate such holidays as *Shabbat*, Pessah, Hanukkah, and Purim.

Take, for example, Purim's famous pastry – the *hamantasch*. Not only did the bakers make a tricornered pocket of dough filled with prunes or poppy seeds, but they noticed that the pinched corners of the pastry resembled an ear. When they spoke Hebrew, they called it an אֹזֶן־הָמָן (*ozen-haman*), "Haman's ear," and thus made a contribution to both the culinary arts and the Hebrew language.

Whether the bakers were making a theological statement about ears is a question shrouded in mystery. Nevertheless, the derivations of the root אזן (ALEF, ZAYIN, NUN) lead us to interesting insights about the organ of hearing.

The Torah uses the root hundreds of times in both literal and metaphorical contexts. Two of the most powerful rhetorical flourishes in all of Scripture have to do with hearing. The first words of Moses' discourse in Deuteronomy are addressed to God: הַאֲזִינוּ הַשָּׁמַיִם וַאֲדַבֵּרָה (*ha'azinu ha-shamayim va-adaberah*), "Hearken, O heavens, and I shall speak." The Psalmist derides idolatry by observing that statues make no sense because they lack sensorial perception: אָזְנַיִם לָהֶם וְלֹא יִשְׁמָעוּ (*oznayim la-hem ve-lo yishma'u*), "They have ears but do not hear."

Readers will recognize in the word אָזְנַיִם (*oznayim*) the rule that the plural for parts of the body that come in pairs – for example, hands, legs, eyes, and ears -- ends in ־יִם (*-ayim*). Interestingly, the same is true for the Hebrew word for scales, מֹאזְנַיִם (*moznayim*), which also contains our root. Is it possible that the biblical writer who told us that we must have מֹאזְנֵי־צֶדֶק (*moznei-tsedek*), honest scales, also knew something about the anatomy of the ear where the cochlea affects equilibrium?

In modern Hebrew, we recognize the value of אִזּוּן (*izun*), "balance." Sometimes, when discretion is in order, you don't want to talk too loudly. After all, as they say in the spy novels, אָזְנַיִם לַכֹּתֶל (*oznayim la-kotel*), "The wall has ears." People in Israel who listen to the radio — and that means almost everyone — are politely addressed by the announcer as מַאֲזִינִים יְקָרִים (*ma'azinim yekarim*), "dear listeners."

If all you want to do is celebrate Purim at its proper season and with the proper food, then eat another אֹזֶנְמָן (*ozenman*), as some Israelis have shortened it. Whether you eat prune or poppy, you will be reminding tyrants the world over that justice comes in all shapes and flavors and may even come from strudel makers.

2

אחד

ALEF, HET, DALET

ONE BY ONE

Sometimes, but unfortunately not always, an effective way of addressing a social or political problem is to try to understand its underlying semantic complexity. Take, for example, the prickly issue of Jewish unity.

We are all certain that we know what we mean when we talk of אַחְדּוּת (*ahdut*), "unity," or when we repeat the slogan עַם אֶחָד (*am ehad*), "one people." Often, however, we fail to take into consideration the meanings that the person we are talking to, or Jewish history for that matter, associates with these words and phrases.

The word אֶחָד (*ehad*), "one," in traditional Jewish ideology is usually reserved not for the Jewish people but for God, as in the *Shema* prayer, the universal Jewish declaration of faith in God's oneness, otherwise known as monotheism. In the Jewish textual tradition, the word אֶחָד (*ehad*) means not only "one" but also "first." In the biblical account of the creation of the world, the first day is called not יוֹם רִאשׁוֹן (*yom rishon*), as we might expect and as it is called elsewhere, but יוֹם אֶחָד (*yom ehad*). A good midrashist who is also a bit of a cynic might read into the use of the cardinal number אֶחָד (*ehad*), instead of the ordinal number רִאשׁוֹן (*rishon*), a moment of hesitation on God's part as to whether He ought to continue with the rest of creation.

One thing the Rabbis were not cynical about was Jewish marriage. The rabbinic expression אֶחָד בְּשַׁבָּת (*ehad be-shabbat*), the first day of the week, is found on *ketubbot*, Jewish marriage contracts, given when the ceremony takes place on a Saturday night or a Sunday.

In Israel, the root אחד (ALEF, HET, DALET) finds its way into some colorful idioms and constructions. To direct people to enter a room "one by one," you simply double our word and say הִכָּנְסוּ אֶחָד אֶחָד (*hikansu ehad ehad*). Would you trust someone who is אֶחָד בַּפֶּה וְאֶחָד בַּלֵּב

(*ehad ba-peh ve-ehad ba-lev*), whose mouth says something different from what his heart feels?

In Hebrew slang, when the word אֶחָד (*ehad*) is used after a positive noun, the noun's meaning is changed to a pejorative one. For example, when you speak of מוּמְחֶה אֶחָד (*mumheh ehad*) or חָכָם אֶחָד (*hakham ehad*), you are not speaking of an expert or a wise person, but rather of a "so-called expert" and, in the latter case, of a jerk.

By far the most useful form of the root is its combining form חַד (*had*). A one-way street in Israel is חַד־סִטְרִי (*had-sitri*) and an unambiguous statement is חַד־מַשְׁמָעִי (*had-mashma'i*). Mononucleosis, חַד־גַּרְעִינִיּוּת (*had-gar'iniut*), the "kissing disease" that affects the *gar'in*, or nucleus, of the cell, is also found in Israel. So are, despite what you might read in the newspapers or see in Israeli films, relationships that are חַד־זִוּוּגִי (*had zivugi*), "monogamous." Both of these expressions imply that one has not been engaged in a חַד־שִׂיחַ (*had-siah*), "monologue."

Our cynical midrashist might say that the only way to be sure that we speak unambiguously of Jewish unity is to engage in monologue, but let's hope that the Hebrew language will show a better way.

3

אחז

ALEF, HET, ZAYIN

POSSESSION, PERCENT, AND THE LORE

One of the most attractive "Main Streets" in small-town Israel is Ra'anana's Ahuzza Street. The name, meaning "possession," requires historical elucidation. Early on, it seems, plots of land were sold to Zionists abroad so that they might have an אֲחֻזָּה (*ahuzzah*), ownership of a piece of property, in the Land of Israel. In this way, it may be said that these early landowners emulated their forefather Abraham who, having been promised the Land of Canaan by God as an אֲחֻזַּת עוֹלָם (*ahuzzat olam*), inheritance for all eternity, staked his claim to the Land by insisting on paying for an אֲחֻזַּת קֶבֶר (*ahuzzat kever*), an eternal burial place, for his wife, Sarah, and, eventually, for himself and his descendants.

The noun comes from the verbal root אחז (ALEF, HET, ZAYIN), "to hold." The most famous biblical use of the verb has to do with the story of the Binding of Isaac and of the ram who was נֶאֱחַז בַּסְּבַךְ בְּקַרְנָיו (*ne'ehaz ba-sevakh be-karnav*), "caught by its horns in the brambles." The most romantic use of the verb occurs in the Song of Songs. When the lover has finally found her beloved, she announces proudly אֲחַזְתִּיו וְלֹא אַרְפֶּנּוּ (*ahaztiv ve-lo arpenu*), "I took hold of him and will not loose my grasp."

In the Jewish legal system, the classical case dealing with property rights can be found in the most widely studied tractate of the Talmud, *Bava Metzia*, which begins with the words שְׁנַיִם אוֹחֲזִין בְּטַלִּית (*shenayim ohazin be-tallit*), dealing with the case of two people who are holding on to the same garment, thereby claiming ownership of it. (The careful reader will note that the last letter of our verb in this expression is a NUN. This indicates an Aramaic transformation of the word. Why the other two words retain their Hebrew constructions while ours does not is something of a mystery.)

A picturesque idiom to describe deceit is אֲחִיזַת עֵינַיִם (*ahizat einayim*), the "holding" of someone's eyes. In modern Hebrew slang, someone who can't get past the first page of a densely written book might complain אֲנִי עֲדַיִן אוֹחֵז בַּדַּף הָרִאשׁוֹן (*ani ada'in ohez ba-daf ha-rishon*), "I'm still 'holding' on the first page."

One of the most surprising derivatives of our root is the Hebrew word for percentage, אֲחוּזִים (*ahuzim*). Originally, when you said עֶשְׂרִים אֲחֻזִים (*esrim ahuzim*) for 20 percent, you probably meant עֶשְׂרִים אֲחֻזִים מִמֵּאָה (*esrim ahuzim mi-me'ah*), twenty "taken" from one hundred. Today, the word for percent is found almost exclusively without the plural ending. One of the expressions most frequently heard in the animated conversations on the streets of any city in Israel, including Ra'anana, is מֵאָה אָחוּז (*me'ah ahuz*), literally 100 percent, but which to an Israeli means "I agree completely," "No problem," "Whatever you say," "Okay, I'll do it."

With such an expression in *your* vocabulary, it would be easy to take part in a Hebrew conversation, don't you agree? Of course you do. מֵאָה אָחוּז (*me'ah ahuz*).

4

אמן

ALEF, MEM, NUN

TRUTH AND BEAUTY

In addition to everything else they do, words can be ambassadors of goodwill, spreading the messages of a culture. Just as the English word "jeans" (All right, "jeans" is not originally an English word, but let's not quibble.) and all it implies about the American ethos can be found wherever one travels, so, too, the little Hebrew word אָמֵן (amen) can be found in over one thousand other languages, telling the world about one of the essences of Jewish civilization.

What exactly is this essence? Affirmation. The word אָמֵן (amen) is so popular, perhaps, because it is the affirmative response one pronounces upon hearing a blessing. The word's closest equivalent can be found in modern American slang. The expression "Right on" is, believe it or not, probably most proximate to the original sense of the root אמן (ALEF, MEM, NUN), which, as a verb, meant "to array in a straight line."

As the word travels down Jewish history, it takes on new forms and meanings. The Purim story records one of these earlier meanings: to set a child straight by giving him or her both an education and an upbringing. The verb אָמַן (aman) means to tutor, to teach, to bring up. In the Book of Esther it is recorded that Mordecai was Hadassah's אוֹמֵן (omen, accent on the second syllable), the person who brought her up, her tutor.

The road from tutor to artist is a short one. Those who affirm that medicine is an art will turn to their רוֹפֵא אָמָּן (rofe amman), "medical specialist," for his or her expertise and skill. Painting and sculpture, two types of אָמָּנוּת (ommanut), "art," merely require skills and expertise of a different order.

The frequently used Hebrew question הַאֻמְנָם (ha-umnam), meaning "Is that so?" will help us to explore another rich vein in our verbal mine. In the declarative, אָמְנָם (*omnam*) means "in truth" and truth, אֱמֶת (*emet*), is what we're all looking for, especially in the beauty of art.

It appears that אֱמֶת (*emet*) comes from an earlier word, אֱמֶנֶת (*emenet*), based on our root. The little letter נ (*nun*) has a habit of falling off words, and it fell off this one too, to give us אֱמֶת (*emet*). One can still see traces of this נ in נֶאֱמָן (*ne'eman*), "true to one's word," "trustworthy," and in the way Israelis refer to the Geneva Convention as אֲמָנַת גֶ׳נֵבָה (*amanat dzhenevah*).

What is true is what one believes in. To ask someone to present his philosophical credo is to ask for one's אֲנִי מַאֲמִין (*ani ma'amin*), "This is what I believe."

The most successful of the Zionist thinkers, because his plan came to fruition, was Eliezer Ben Yehuda. His credo was that the Jewish nation could not long endure without Hebrew as its living language. He also believed that it was possible to revivify Hebrew and make it the language of the modern Jewish nation in Israel. All who agree that he was right please signify by responding אָמֵן (*amen*).

5

בחר

VET, HET, RESH

THE CHOSEN LANGUAGE

Citizens of the United States and of Israel share a ritual common to all democracies. America votes in quadrennial presidential elections; Israelis choose a prime minister and other Knesset members in their בְּחִירוֹת (*behirot*). This Hebrew word for elections comes from the verb בָּחַר (*bahar*), "He chose."

The Torah uses this verb repeatedly when it speaks of God choosing His people; it also uses the same verb to describe the Israelites' action of choosing God. Interestingly, the classical Hebrew term for "The Chosen People" is not הָעָם הַנִּבְחָר (*ha-am ha-nivhar*) but rather Deuteronomy's expression עַם סְגוּלָה (*am segulah*), "a precious nation." Prayers recited at Jewish festival services do use the root בחר (VET, HET, RESH) when they – and we – proclaim אַתָּה בְחַרְתָּנוּ מִכָּל הָעַמִּים (*atah vehartanu mi-kol ha-amim*), "You have chosen us from among the nations."

The Jews have not only political elections; they also have metaphysical ones. This nation, whose ethos and very survival are built on a system of obligations, is nevertheless told that it has בְּחִירָה חָפְשִׁית (*behirah hofshit*), the liberty to choose between right and wrong. Although all Jews are obliged to marry, they nevertheless have romantic choices – what the poets call elective affinities – as well. Hebrew wedding invitations will often describe the bride as בְּחִירַת לִבּוֹ (*behirat libo*), "the choice of [the bridegroom's] heart."

Two vernacular nouns using our root are בָּחוּר (*bahur*) and בַּחוּרָה (*bahurah*), "young man" and "young woman." How did we get from chosenness to youthfulness? A phrase in 1 Samuel, בַּחוּרֵי יִשְׂרָאֵל (*bahurei yisrael*), "chosen of Israel" – describing outstanding young men, "handpicked" to serve in the armed forces – provides an obvious clue.

That the sense of youthfulness is a venerable one is attested to by a phrase in Ecclesiastes urging the enjoyment of "the days of your youth, יְמֵי בַּחֲרוֹתֶיךָ (*yemei bahurotekha*). Second Samuel tells of a town called בַּחוּרִים (*bahurim*), where, presumably, young men dwelled. In Yiddish, the noun בָּחוּר (*bokhr*) is used both for a *yeshivah* student and any unmarried man, whatever his age.

Choosing often implies choosing between two equals, as in מִבְחָר (*mivhar*) and מֻבְחָר (*muvhar*), both of which mean "the best." The former can be found in expressions such as מִבְחָר שִׁירֵי יְמֵי הַבֵּינַיִם (*mivhar shirei yemai ha-beinayim*), "anthology of medieval poetry." The latter noun carries the sense of "best of the best," especially in the expression מִין הַמֻּבְחָר (*min ha-muvhar*), "choicest."

A finicky chooser is called a בַּחֲרָן (*baharan*). When it comes to elections — whether political, affective, or metaphysical — choosy sounds like a good thing to be.

6

בטח

VET, TET, HET

WHAT'S SURE IS SECURE

Sometimes one word – repeated so often in the media that one begins to feel it reflects a universal concern – will by itself define the *Zeitgeist*, the spirit of the times. A good case might be made that what we're all concerned about these days is security.

The Hebrew word for security, בִּטָּחוֹן (*bitahon*), is heard most often with reference to the United Nations מוֹעֶצֶת הַבִּטָּחוֹן (*mo'etzet ha-bitahon*), Security Council, or to Israel's שַׂר הַבִּטָּחוֹן (*sar ha-bitahon*), minister of defense.

The original meaning of the root בטח (VET, TET, HET) is "to lie extended on the ground." How do we get from there to the notion of security? One way of showing that one feels secure is to "rest easy."

One of the most famous phrases in all of Scripture has to do not with lying down, perhaps, but with sitting securely, לָבֶטַח (*la-vetah*), under one's vine and fig tree. And speaking of vines and of lying on the ground, there are those who believe that the Hebrew word for watermelon, אֲבַטִּיחַ (*avatiah*), comes from our root.

In Judaism, security and praise of God are always intertwined. That might be the reason that the mnemonic device for remembering when the Full Hallel is recited is ב״בטח (*be"vetah*), in which the letters stand for the numbers 2, 2, 9, and 8. One says the Full Hallel on the first two days of Passover, on the two days of Shavuot, on the nine days of Sukkot, and on the eight days of Hanukkah. Good Zionists will also say Full Hallel on Yom ha-Atzma'ut and Yom Yerushalayim, two more celebrations of Jewish security. The verb בָּטַח (*batah*), in the sense of "to place one's trust in," is applied in Scripture to God, with one meaningful exception: the Woman of Valor, about whom it is said בָּטַח בָּהּ לֵב בַּעְלָהּ (*batah bah lev ba'lah*), "Her husband places his trust in *her*."

Nowadays, the way we provide financial security for our family is to take out an insurance policy, תְּעוּדַת בִּטּוּחַ (*te'udat bituah*). One also hears our root in the verb לְהַבְטִיחַ (*le-havtiah*), "to promise." The connection between security and promising can be found in a prophetic song of a few years ago in which a singer-soldier croons אֲנִי מַבְטִיחַ לָךְ (*ani mavtiah lakh*), "I promise you," to his little daughter, reassuring her that *this* will be the last war.

To say that a bird in the hand is worth two in the bush, you need only repeat מַה שֶׁבָּטוּחַ בָּטוּחַ (*mah she-batuah batuah*), "What's sure is sure." And then there is the two-syllable reassurance בֶּטַח (*betah*), "Of course!" which most Israelis use and which those who hear it have learned to be wary of. But then again, wariness, like security, is also part of the *Zeitgeist*.

7
בטל

VET, TET, LAMED

A LOAFER IN THE CITY

If you were to ask Teddy Kollek, the former mayor of Jerusalem, or Shlomo Lahat, the erstwhile mayor of Tel Aviv, what distinguishes a city from a village, you can be sure that either of them would be able to tick off the names of dozens of cultural attractions, architectural landmarks, or shopping and eating emporia. Pose the same question to someone immersed in Jewish text and he or she would quote the Talmud: a city exists when it has עֲשָׂרָה בַּטְלָנִים (asarah batlanim), "ten loafers."

What the Talmud means is that any city worthy of the name should have at least ten men of leisure who have chosen to pursue a scholarly life and who are always available to form a *minyan* at a moment's notice.

Speaking of scholarly pursuits, there is a Greek expression used to characterize a word that appears only once in Scripture: a *hapax legomenon*. It is of more than passing interest that the root בטל (VET, TET, LAMED), which is used in dozens of expressions in rabbinic literature, appears only once in the Hebrew Bible. In Ecclesiastes, the Preacher warns וּבָטְלוּ הַטֹּחֲנוֹת (u-vatlu ha-tohanot), literally, "the grinders shall cease," metaphorically, "your teeth will fall out."

The Rabbis use the expression בָּטֵל בְּשִׁשִּׁים (batel be-shishim) to signify that the essence of a substance becomes neutralized when immersed in sixty parts of another substance. The expression עוֹבֵר בָּטֵל (over batel), which in Hebrew means the same thing as בַּטְלָן (batlan), "an idler," is used in Yiddish to describe someone who has become senile. In Yiddish, it sounds something like *iberbutl*.

No less than Yiddish, modern Hebrew is a spoken language that likes to dress its classical expressions in modern garb. The Rabbis taught that if you make a blessing over a piece of fruit, for example, and then don't eat the fruit, you have made a בְּרָכָה לְבַטָּלָה (berakhah le-

vatalah), a blessing in vain. Today in Israel, any wasted speech or action, like trying to convince a deadbeat to repay the shekels he owes you, is also called a בְּרָכָה לְבַטָּלָה (*berakhah le-vatalah*).

The root בטל (VET, TET, LAMED) also shows how modern speakers of the language use Hebrew to preserve Aramaic. A scholarly article on labor relations, for example, might report that a הַבְטָלָה (*havtalah*), "a lockout of the workers," has led, directly or indirectly to אַבְטָלָה (*avtalah*), unemployment. In both cases, in the Hebrew and the Aramaic forms, the workers have become בַּטְלָנִים (*batlanim*).

Not long ago, two Israeli comedians, Natan Datner and Avi Kushnir by name, stars of the Beersheva Acting Company, entered the pre-Eurovision song contest in Israel, performing שִׁיר הַבַּטְלָנִים (*shir ha-batlanim*), "The Loafers' Song." That they won the contest is testimony to David Ben-Gurion's contention that Beersheva is a city on a par with Jerusalem and Tel Aviv.

8

בִּין

VET, YOD, NUN

A WORD FOR THE WISE

Not too long ago William Safire, the self-proclaimed language maven of the *New York Times*, was asked about the origin of the word maven, which came to Safire's English via Yiddish. Safire – preferring rather to dilate on such notions as pundits, boffins, and opinion leaders – deftly avoided answering the question. The challenge, however, is worth taking up.

The Hebrew verb מֵבִין (*mevin*, accent on the second syllable) is the masculine singular in the present tense of the infinitive לְהָבִין (*le-havin*), "to understand." In modern colloquial Hebrew, it too is used as a noun having the Yiddish, and now English, meaning of "expert." The word comes from the three-letter root בין (VET, YOD, NUN), which originally meant to pierce. A person who can intellectually pierce through to the meaning of a difficult concept obviously has הֲבָנָה (*havanah*), "understanding." Such a person is also able to distinguish between truth and falsehood. Thus the existence of the much-used Hebrew preposition בֵּין (*bein*), "between."

Some of the more confusing nouns deriving from בין are בִּינָה (*binah*), "insight"; תְּבוּנָה (*tevuna*), "reason"; בִּיּוּן (*biyyun*), "intelligence"; and נָבוֹן (*navon*), "wise" and "reasonable." Of course, or as they say in Hebrew, כַּמּוּבָן (*ka-muvan*), the noun נָבוֹן (*navon*) is instantly recognized by those who remember fondly the wise and reasonable former president of the State of Israel, Yitzhak Navon.

The name of the educational arm of the Lubavitcher hasidic movement, Habad, is an acronym for חָכְמָה, בִּינָה, דַּעַת (*hokhmah, binah, da'at*), "wisdom, insight, and understanding." These near synonyms risk rendering this discussion less and less מוּבָן (*muvan*), "understood," by the reader, thus justifying Safire's avoidance of the question.

A maven of reading for comprehension, הֲבָנַת הַנִּקְרָא (*havanat ha-nikra*), would perhaps find it profitable to move on to another family of

---

words, related to the preposition בֵּין (*bein*), "between." The Middle Ages, יְמֵי־הַבֵּינַיִם (*yemei ha-beinayim*), were a time when the middle class, הַמַּעֲמָד הַבֵּינוֹנִי (*ha-ma'amad ha-beinoni*), of the Jewish people flourished. Today, as in the Middle Ages, the influence of the Jews is felt on a scale that can rightly be classified as בֵּינְלְאֻמִי (*beinle'umi*), "international." While Jews have often been moderate, rarely have they been mediocre. In either case, you would use the adjective בֵּינוֹנִי (*beinoni*), "average."

Strictly between us, בֵּינֵינוּ לְבֵין עַצְמֵינוּ (*beneinu le-vein atsmeinu*), did you know that the word מֵבִין (*mevin*) appears in the Bible in what may be a variation of Safire's sense? Nehemiah 8:3 reports that Ezra, called the "Sofer," the maker of books (and the origin, by the way, of Safire's name), read the Torah before a public described as הָאֲנָשִׁים וְהַנָּשִׁים וְהַמְּבִינִים (*ha-anashim, ve-ha-nashim, ve-ha-mevinim*), "the men, the women, and the mavens." Who are these "mavens," a third gender? Not very likely. The chronicler must have had a different meaning in mind, perhaps something like "those who would understand."

In any case, Safire might be wise to choose a different title for himself. Jewish tradition and the Hebrew language provide the perfect word, פּוֹסֵק (*posek*), "decisor," designating one who, by common consent, is authorized to render legal decisions. For more about this highly respected title, see chapter 67.

9

בקר

VET, KOF, RESH

A DISTINCTION WITH A DIFFERENCE

In Jewish thought, evening and morning are polar opposites, not only temporally but also philosophically. Evening, as is explained in chapter 61, is a time for mixing together, for creating confusions. Morning, on the other hand, is a time when one is able to make distinctions, one of the essences of Judaism. The word בֹּקֶר (*boker,* accent on the first syllable), "morning," together with its cognates, comes from a root that literally means "to make distinctions."

As a verb, בִּקֵּר (*bikker*) means "to investigate," "to examine." A בִּקֹּרֶת (*bikoret*) can be a scientific investigation, an analysis of a work of art, or a book review in which one points up the distinctive characteristics of a work. Sometimes a language will create a word even though the culture will have very limited use for the concept. A hypercritical, censorious person, for example, is said to be בַּקְרָנִי (*bakrani*).

In a second sense, the verb בִּקֵּר (*bikker*) means "to visit." One of the most highly prized *mitzvot* of Judaism is בִּיקוּר חוֹלִים (*bikur holim*), "the visiting of the sick." The use of the verb בִּקֵּר (*bikker*) in this sense stems perhaps from one's intention to distinguish the signs of a patient's recovery. Curiously, the French expression *visiter un malade* means not to visit the sick but "to examine a patient," presumably to make medical distinctions.

The verb לְבַקֵּר (*le-vakker*) is also used in circumstances that involve going somewhere, like לְבַקֵּר בְּבֵית הַסֵּפֶר (*le-vakker be-veit ha-sefer*), "to attend school," or לְבַקֵּר בַּתֵּאַטרוֹן (*le-vakker ba-te'atron*), "to go to the theater."

One of the most curious cognates of the root בקר (VET, KOF, RESH) is the noun for cattle, בָּקָר (*bakar*). One scholar has suggested that, as a plowing ox makes furrows in the earth, it distinguishes for the farmer the place where the seed may be most profitably placed. This language investigator relates בָּקַר (bakar) to both בָּקַע (baka) and בָּצַע (batsa), both of which mean "to split."

Perhaps we ought also to look at the modern Hebrew word for cowboy, בּוֹקֵר (boker, accent on the second syllable). It comes from a word found only once in Scripture. The prophet Amos is not merely a shepherd but also a בּוֹקֵר (boker), one who oversees the flock, observing closely that he has the right count — an investigator, after all.

One of the most beautiful uses of the verb לְבַקֵּר (le-vakker), in its sense of distinction-making, is in the expression לְבַקֵּר בֵּין טוֹב לָרָע (le-vakker bein tov la-ra), "to distinguish between good and evil." It's not always easy to do so. But we all know a בֹּקֶר טוֹב (boker tov) when we see one. Isn't it amazing that just by saying בֹּקֶר טוֹב (boker tov), we can create a good morning?

10

ברך

BET, RESH, KHAF

AT THE KNEES

How is prayer like the game of basketball? To succeed at either, you have to concentrate and, at the opportune moment, to bend your knees.

That the Hebrew word for knee, בֶּרֶךְ (*berekh*, accent on the first syllable), is at the root of the word for blessing, בְּרָכָה (*berakhah*), suggests that the essence of the very spiritual activity of prayer is indeed a very physical act – kneeling.

It goes without saying that the words בְּרָכָה (*berakhah*) and בָּרוּךְ (*barukh*) are among the most frequently used in Jewish religious life. In the prayer book, בָּרוּךְ (*barukh*) is the first word of every blessing. The name of the first tractate of the Talmud, dealing with the laws of prayer, is בְּרָכוֹת (*berakhot*), the plural of בָּרוּךְ (*barukh*). The word is also familiar in many compounds. Grace after meals is בִּרְכַּת הַמָּזוֹן (*birkat ha-mazon*); the priestly blessing is בִּרְכַּת כֹּהֲנִים (*birkat kohanim*).

A living language like Hebrew will, of course, update venerable usages in colorful ways. Thus בָּרוּךְ שֶׁפְּטָרַנִי (*barukh she-petarani*), the formula releasing parents from responsibility for children who have reached the age of *mitzvot*, becomes in modern Hebrew "Good riddance" when a *nudnik* finally takes leave. The expression בְּרָכָה לְבַטָּלָה (*berakhah le-vatalah*), describing a "blessing in vain," said when a blessing is neither required nor permitted, is used in colloquial speech to characterize all wasted effort.

One of the most fascinating uses of the root ברך (VET, RESH, KHAF) is found in the title given by the Egyptians to the young man who had dreamt that his brothers and parents would one day kneel before him. Joseph is addressed as אַבְרֵךְ (*avrekh*), probably from a salutation like "Hail," accompanied perhaps by the slight genuflection made when one is in the presence of nobility. In modern Hebrew an אַבְרֵךְ (*avrekh*) is a young gentleman-scholar, otherwise known as a yeshiva boy.

And what of the word בְּרֵכָה (berekhah), meaning a man-made "pool" or "pond"? To walk into a pool of water that reaches the knees, מֵי בִרְכַּיִם (mei birkayim), is to walk into a בְּרֵכָה (berekhah). A בְּרֵכָה (berekhah) might also be a place where one causes an animal — a camel, for example — to kneel in order to drink water. A more adventurous but equally plausible explanation takes its cue from the verb בָּרַךְ (barakh), "to hollow out": a בְּרֵכָה (berekhah) is a hollowed-out receptacle for water.

Whether speculative or not, the search for the origins of our word is made easier by concentrating — with or without genuflection — on the three little letters of its root.

II

גאל

GIMMEL, ALEF, LAMED

REDEEMING VALUE

How do we know that redemption is central to Jewish culture? Not necessarily from the number of words derived from the root גאל (GIMMEL, ALEF, LAMED), "to redeem" – there are only a handful of these. Rather, redemption's centrality comes from the high frequency of use and the wide variety of places in which the verb גָּאַל (*ga'al*), "He redeemed," and the nouns גּוֹאֵל (*go'el*), "redeemer," and גְּאוּלָה (*ge'ulah*), "redemption," appear.

Sometimes, in fact, the same phrase using a form of our root will appear in more than one genre of Jewish literature. The phrase, for example, with which the patriarch Jacob blesses his grandsons, Joseph's sons, Ephraim and Menashe, הַמַּלְאָךְ הַגֹּאֵל אֹתִי מִכָּל רָע (*ha-malakh ha-go'el oti mi-kol ra*), "The angel who redeems me from all evil," will turn up later as a liturgical text surrounding the bedtime recitation of the *Shema* and, even more recently, in a lullaby sung by Jewish mothers who really believe in early-childhood education.

The root is also found in proper names in modern Israel. Witness the names of the famous archaeologist-soldier, יְגָאֵל יָדִין, Yigal Yadin, and the singer, גְּאוּלָה גִיל Geulah Gill.

Originally, the verb גָּאַל (*ga'al*) meant "to buy back." Interestingly, that is also the original meaning of the English word "redemption." Since the *emptor* in the Latin expression *Caveat emptor* is the famous "buyer who should beware," a "buyer back" in Latin would be a "re-(d)emptor."

In the Torah, the term גּוֹאֵל (*go'el*) is used to designate a relative. This comes from the ancient practice of גְּאוּלַת דָּם (*ge'ulat dam*), a blood revenge exacted for the murder of a close relative. Later, the term גּוֹאֵל (*go'el*) came to mean "someone who marries the childless widow of a close relative" and therefore "redeems" his name from oblivion.

The most famous of these redemptions – triggered by the decla-

---

ration אִם יִגְאָלֵךְ טוֹב יִגְאָל (*im yig'alekh tov yig'al*), "If he redeems you, good, let him redeem" — is one that did not take place. The Book of Ruth relates that since Ruth's mother-in-law Naomi's nearest living relative did not wish to perform his redemptive duty, and thereby turned down the opportunity to go down in midrashic Jewish history as טוֹב (*tov*), "good," it was left to old man Boaz to marry Ruth. He thereby become with her the progenitor of King David, from whose line the Redeemer of Righteousness, the גּוֹאֵל צֶדֶק (*go'el tsedek*), that is, the Messiah, would eventually be born.

It should come as no surprise that Jewish liturgy is replete with prayers for redemption. In the morning service, the entire section between the *Shema* and the *Amidah* prayer is called the גְּאוּלָה (*ge'ulah*), as is the seventh of the eighteen benedictions of the *Amidah* itself.

Perhaps because earning redemption is a task to be undertaken daily, the Prayer for the State of Israel calls the modern Jewish state רֵאשִׁית צְמִיחַת גְּאוּלָתֵנוּ (*reishit tsemihat ge'ulateinu*), "the first flowering of our redemption," thereby stressing, in true Zionist fashion, that it may be more important to work at bringing גְּאוּלָה (*ge'ulah*) than to pray for it.

12

גבר

GIMMEL, VET, RESH

A MAN'S A MAN,
FOR ALL THAT

Sexism aside, one of the more interesting aspects of a language – and especially of the Hebrew language – is the vocabulary dealing with gender. Take, for example, גֶּבֶר (*gever*), one of the Hebrew words for "man."

The root גבר (GIMMEL, VET, RESH) has several connotations having to do with masculinity. To begin with, the Hebrew word for a strutting rooster is the same as that for man, גֶּבֶר (*gever*). That noun also means both "male reproductive organ" and "hero," obviously betraying a correspondence between the two in the mind of ancient man.

In Israel, high school girls discussing their favorite television programs with their classmates could, not long ago, be overheard referring to the macho hero of the "MacGyver" series as "My *Gever*," always followed by a sigh.

The modern word for hero is גִּבּוֹר (*gibbor*), a noun that in the Bible is paired in Homeric style with the name of strongman Samson: שִׁמְשׁוֹן הַגִּבּוֹר (*shimshon ha-gibbor*). The Mishna softens the concept of heroism somewhat when, to the question אֵיזֶהוּ גִבּוֹר (*eizehu gibbor*), "Who is a hero?" it answers, "One who conquers his own inclinations."

The verb גָּבַר (*gavar*) means, "to be strong," "to conquer," "to win." In the biblical battle with Israel's archenemy Amalek, related in Exodus, chapter 17, we are told that all Moses had to do was to raise his hand, וְגָבַר יִשְׂרָאֵל (*ve-gavar yisrael*), "and Israel would prevail." Nowadays, the same verb is found on the sports pages of Israeli newspapers, with the journalist reporting how Maccabi-Tel Aviv's team גָּבְרָה עַל (*gavrah al*), "defeated" the team of Hapoel-Ramat Gan.

The reflexive form of the verb, לְהִתְגַּבֵּר (*le-hitgabber*), is prevalent in the spoken language. A raw army recruit learns quickly לְהִתְגַּבֵּר עַל

קְשָׁיִים (*le-hitgabber al keshayim*), "to surmount difficulties," the least of which may be that he had to leave behind his stereo with its מַגְבֵּר (*mag-ber*), "amplifier."

Names can also tell interesting stories. One of the angels who will accompany the redemption is called גַבְרִיאֵל (*gavriel*), literally, and very mystically, "My man is God." It is no small curiosity that the Romance languages' form of this manly name, Gabriel, has a feminine equivalent in both its French and Italian versions, Gabrielle and Gabriella. Wonder of wonders, the polite form of feminine address used in Hebrew for both Mrs. and Miss — thus obviating the need for Hebrew to create an equivalent to Ms. — is the word גְבֶרֶת (*geveret*).

Sometimes the language itself will set sexism aside.

13
גלל

GIMMEL, LAMED, LAMED

ROLL 'EM

One of the lessons we learn from the Passover liturgy is that Purim's Book of Esther is not Judaism's only מְגִלָּה (*megillah*), scroll. There are four other biblical מְגִלּוֹת (*megillot*), including the Song of Songs, which is read on the intermediate *Shabbat* of Passover. Although not all synagogues read from a rolled-up and subsequently unfolded scroll, rolling and unfolding are the meanings inherent in *megillah*'s root, גלל (GIMMEL, LAMED, LAMED).

Originally the verb גָּלַל (*galal*) meant to roll large stones, and in the Bible the verb often comes attached to the noun אֶבֶן (*even*), stone. A גַּל אֲבָנִים (*gal avanim*), a "pile of stones," was often crafted together to form a statue, an idol for worship, hence the line in the *aleinu* prayer, לְהַעֲבִיר גִּלּוּלִים מִן הָאָרֶץ (*le-ha'avir gillulim min ha-arets*), "to cause the idols to pass."

An insight into the way political districts were formed in ancient Israel comes from our root as well. It should not be surprising to learn that the word for district, or circuit, is גָּלִיל (*galil*), and that what we know today as *the* Galilee, was the big district known as הַגָּלִיל (*ha-galil*).

Rolling usually applies to round things, as in one of the nouns for "pill," גְּלוּלָה (*gelulah*). When the ocean's tide rolls in, it forms גַּלִּים (*gal-lim*), "waves." And when sound waves accumulate in Israel, we get music, news, and commentary, as in the name of the Israel Defense Force's radio station, גַּלֵּי צַהַ"ל (*gallei tsahal*), which features, by the way, a fascinating segment on the Hebrew language, Avshalom Kor's רֶגַע שֶׁל עִבְרִית (*rega shel ivrit*), "a minute of Hebrew."

Hebrew speakers don't have to reinvent the wheel every time they create a new word. Sometimes they will just double what they have, as in גַּלְגַּל (*galgal*), "wheel," a thing rolled over and over. Jews, who know that history repeats itself, will, if they speak modern Hebrew, tell you

---

that גַּלְגַּל חוֹזֵר בָּעוֹלָם (*galgal hozer ba-olam*), "The wheel of fortune always comes around full circle."

If English has the graphic expression "heads will roll," Hebrew goes it one better: one of the words for head in Hebrew is גֻּלְגּוֹלֶת (*gulgolet*), a nicely rounded skull. Even those who don't believe in rolling heads might be tempted by the doctrine of the "rolling (transmigration) of the souls," גִּלְגּוּל הַנֶּפֶשׁ (*gilgul ha-nefesh*), "metempsychosis."

We are all taught that it's important to "get the ball rolling," implying in this motion a relation of cause to effect. When the Torah wishes to explain the prosperity of the House of Potiphar in Egypt, it tells us that it was prosperous, בִּגְלַל יוֹסֵף (*biglal yosef*), "on account of Joseph." From the Exodus from Egypt, celebrated during the month of *Nisan*, to the מְגִלַּת הַעַצְמָאוּת (*megillat ha-atsma'ut*), the "Proclamation of Independence" of the State of Israel, celebrated during the following month of *Iyyar*, is but a stone's roll. *Hag same'ah*, all around.

14
גרש

GIMMEL, RESH, SHIN

1492 AND ALL THAT

At the beginning of 1992, Jews the world over, aided by a properly contrite Spanish government, began commemorating the 500th anniversary of the expulsion of the Jews from Spain.

While English and Spanish language mavens were moved at that juncture to ponder in print the sources of words like "quincentennial" or "Marrano," Hebrew language lovers rushed to consider the roots and shoots of the Hebrew expression for this event, גֵּרוּשׁ סְפָרַד (gerush sefarad).

This expression echoes two earlier expulsions in Jewish history. When the Torah recounts that Adam and Eve were expelled from the Garden of Eden, it uses our root, גרש (GIMMEL, RESH, SHIN), to narrate the event, וַיְגָרֶשׁ אֶת הָאָדָם (va-yegaresh et ha-adam), "and so He drove man out." When the Bible wishes to explain why we eat matzot to commemorate the Exodus, it explains כִּי גֹרְשׁוּ מִמִּצְרַיִם (ki gorshu mi-mitsrayim), "because they were driven out of Egypt" (and didn't have time to let the dough of their bread rise).

The root is also used in Jewish divorce law, called in Aramaic גֵּרוּשִׁין (gerushin). A divorcée is called a גְּרוּשָׁה (gerushah), her erstwhile husband a גָּרוּשׁ (garush). Since in Jewish law the husband initiates the divorce action, he should more properly be called a מְגָרֵשׁ (megaresh), "one who causes a domestic expulsion."

Other usages of the root require a healthy stretch of the imagination. One meaning, to stir up or cause a commotion, is found in the biblical expression for a stormy sea, a יָם נִגְרָשׁ (yam nigrash). Another usage is found in the noun גֶּרֶשׁ (geresh), meaning "fruit" or "produce." This requires the etymological contortions of no less an authority than the eleventh-century Hebrew philologist David Kimhi, who explains the biblical expression גֶּרֶשׁ יְרָחִים (geresh yerahim), "monthly produce," by asserting that there are fruits that are propelled into being by the action of the moon.

Visitors to Israel may well ask how we get to the expression for parking lot, מִגְרַשׁ חֲנָיָה (*migrash hanayah*), from our root. One explanation goes as follows: Since a *migrash* was originally an open space outside of town where animals were "sent out" for grazing, any lot today is called a מִגְרָשׁ (*migrash*). This is also the word for several types of playing fields, including, in Israel, the ubiquitous מִגְרַשׁ כַּדּוּר רֶגֶל (*migrash kadur regel*), "soccer field."

Students of biblical cantillation may well wonder how we get the word גֶּרֶשׁ (*geresh*) as the name for one of the notes. A hint is available from the musical terms "andante" (going forward) and "fugue" (fleeing). Since there are also Hebrew notes called "preceding" (*kadmah*) and "going" (*azlah*), why should there not be one called, playfully, "chasing" (*geresh*)?

In Israeli culture, chasing is related to indolence. When you talk about someone who spends his whole day doing nothing, you say הוּא מְגָרֵשׁ אֶת הַזְּבוּבִים (*hu megaresh et ha-zevuvim*), "He spends his time chasing flies." Even in politically correct circles concerned with animal rights, that has to be a better activity than expelling people.

HEBREWSPEAK

15

דֶּרֶךְ

DALET, RESH, KHAF

ON THE ROAD

During the Gulf War of 1991, a quintessentially Israeli way to relieve the fear of the use of chemical warfare by Iraq was to make macabre jokes. A jarring example was to be found spray-painted on a wall in the village of Kfar Saba: תִּקְנוּ נַקְנִיקִיּוֹת, הַחַרְדָּל בַּדֶּרֶךְ (*tiknu nakni-kiyot, ha-hardal ba-derekh*), "Buy hot dogs, the mustard is on the way." The witticism plays on the double meaning of mustard (spicy condiment and deadly gas) as it introduces one of the richest verbs in the Hebrew language, דָּרַךְ (*darakh*), "to tread."

The root appears in Scripture over 750 times, often in a theological context. Great pathos is revealed in Moses' efforts to understand God. His request, הוֹדִעֵנִי נָא אֶת דְּרָכֶךָ (*hodi'eini na et derakhekha*), "Announce to me Your ways," is refused out of hand. The prophets were also taken with the theological implications of a notion of God's way. The prophet Isaiah, speaking for God, announces לֹא דַרְכֵיכֶם דְּרָכָי (*lo darkheikhem derakhai*), "Your ways are not My ways." And while the prophet Jeremiah asks the Jobian question מַדּוּעַ דֶּרֶךְ רְשָׁעִים צָלֵחָה (*madu'a derekh resha'im tselekhah*), "Why does the way of the wicked prosper?," King David's great faith is demonstrated in his proud assertion, צַדִּיק ה' בְּכָל דְּרָכָיו (*tsaddik ha-shem bekhol derakhav*), "God is just in all His ways."

The Rabbis taught that דֶּרֶךְ אֶרֶץ קָדְמָה לַתּוֹרָה (*derekh erets kadmah la-torah*), "good manners [literally, the way of the earth] take precedence over Torah study," usually, for the Rabbis, the highest good. They also enfolded dozens of biblical phrases into the prayer book using the word דֶּרֶךְ (*derekh*), from the *Shema*'s וּבְלֶכְתְּךָ בַדֶּרֶךְ (*u-velekhtekha va-derekh*), "when you walk upon the road," to the tuneful assertion about the Torah that דְּרָכֶיהָ דַרְכֵי נֹעַם (*derakhehah darkhei no'am*), "Her [the Torah's] ways are the ways of pleasantness."

In modern Israel, the popular way of wishing someone a bon

---

voyage is to exclaim דֶּרֶךְ צְלֵחָה (derekh tselehah), literally "a successful road." In general, or as they say, בְּדֶרֶךְ כְּלָל (be-derekh kelal), or by the way, for that matter, דֶּרֶךְ אַגַּב (derekh aggav), the root comes up at every turn of the road in Israel, as in תַּדְרִיךְ (tadrikh), "briefing," דַּרְכּוֹן (darkon), "passport," מַדְרִיךְ (madrikh), "tourist guide" or "camp counselor," and in your מַדְרִיךְ טֶלֶפוֹן (madrikh telefon), "telephone directory."

The idea of locomotion is found in the words for sidewalk מִדְרָכָה (midrakhah), and for your car's odometer, מַדְּרֶךְ (madderekh), a playful combination of the words מָדַד (madad), to measure, and דֶּרֶךְ (derekh).

When you go on a hike, don't forget to recite the traveler's prayer, תְּפִילַת הַדֶּרֶךְ (tefillat ha-derekh), and to pack your knapsack with צֵידָה לַדֶּרֶךְ (tsedah la-derekh), "supplies for the road," that is, food. You'll take along hot dogs if you have faith, for you'll believe that the condiment that adds spice to life is on the way.

16

הלך

HEH, LAMED, KHAF

ON THE GO

According to Hebrew poet Hayyim Nahman Bialik, a pioneering figure of the Jewish cultural renaissance of the twentieth century, the essence of Jewish culture can be discerned in the play between its two fundamental elements, הֲלָכָה (halakhah) and אַגָּדָה (aggadah), law and lore.

How is it that the noun הֲלָכָה (halakhah), which originally meant "practice," should have taken on the force of a word like "law"? Might we conjecture that we passed from "the way things go" to "the way things ought to go" because the root הלך (HEH, LAMED, KHAF), "to go," "to walk," lends itself so readily to the imperative, that part of speech in which commands are given?

Possibly the most far-reaching command in the Torah is לֶךְ־לְךָ (lekh lekha), "Betake yourself," God's command to Abraham that he leave his birthplace and go to a new homeland. To emphasize a point about possession, God gives another command to Abraham using another form of the root: קוּם הִתְהַלֵּךְ בָּאָרֶץ (kum hithalekh ba-arets), "Arise and walk the [length and breadth of] the land," and thereby, according to ancient Near Eastern law, take possession of it.

The Torah's command against slander and gossip, לֹא תֵלֵךְ רָכִיל (lo telekh rakhil), in using the verb "to go," presents a vivid picture of the slanderer walking to and fro to spread his malice.

Modern Hebrew has adopted the imperative of our verb to express extreme anger, as in the expression לֵךְ לַעֲזָאזֵל (lekh la-azazel), "Go to hell," or the even more forceful לֵךְ כִּיבִּינִימַט (lekh kibinimat), a curious amalgam of Hebrew and Russian-Yiddish that should perhaps be reserved for anti-Semites, so strong is its meaning. Modern Hebrew also uses our verb in the past tense to create a sort of slangy, attenuated imperative, as in הָלַכְנוּ (halakhnu), a figurative transformation of "We went" to "Let's go."

When Theodor Herzl, like Bialik a pioneering figure of the twentieth century's Jewish renaissance, said (not in Hebrew, perhaps, but let's not ruin a good conclusion for a mere detail) אִם תִּרְצוּ אֵין זוֹ אַגָּדָה (*im tirtsu ein zo aggadah*), "If you will it [the creation of a homeland], it is no fable," did he perhaps mean that to have a Jewish state is not אַגָּדָה (*aggadah*), lore, but הֲלָכָה (*halakhah*), law? After all, a Jewish state is both the way things are and the way they ought to be.

17

הפך

HEH, FEH, KHAF

AU CONTRAIRE

Is Hebrew a supernatural language? There are those who believe that there is magic in the letters themselves. After all, they argue, was not the Golem of Prague first fashioned out of earth and water and then brought to life by having three Hebrew letters etched onto his forehead?

Skeptics may disagree, but even Hebrew grammarians – for whom there is a rational explanation for nearly all the capricious vagaries of the language – will not deny that there is something akin to magic in what they call, in Hebrew, the וָו הַהִפּוּךְ (*vav ha-hipukh*) and, in English, "conversive *vav*." This is a letter that turns the past into the future and the future into the past. For example, if you wish to say, as it appears in the Torah countless times, "Moses spoke," you take the future form of the phrase יְדַבֵּר מֹשֶׁה (*yidabber moshe*), "Moses shall speak," add the וָו הַהִפּוּךְ (*vav ha-hipukh*) and, presto changeo, you have וַיְדַבֵּר מֹשֶׁה (*va-yidabber moshe*), "Moses spoke."

Changing one thing into another is accomplished not only by the *va ha-hipukh* but also by using the very root הפך (HEH, FEH, KHAF), "to change," in a rich variety of idiomatic expressions. In modern Israel, if you want to change a cup of espresso into a cup of cappuccino, all you have to do is walk into an Israeli café and ask for קָפֶה הָפוּךְ (*kafeh hafukh*).

In the Bible, the reluctant prophet Jonah walks into the sinful city of Nineveh and proclaims, עוֹד אַרְבָּעִים יוֹם וְנִינְוֵה נֶהְפָּכֶת (*od arbaim yom ve-nineveh neh'pakhet*), "In forty days Nineveh shall be overturned." Of course, that's not exactly what happened. *Au contraire*, or, as they say in Hebrew, לְהֵפֶךְ (*le-hefekh*), the inhabitants of Nineveh repented and the city was spared. Poor Jonah.

The Talmud tells us that Persian King Ahasuerus of the Book of Esther was like many a modern-day Persian Gulf leader – capricious.

They called him a הֲפַכְפְּכָן (*hafakhpekhan*), a person who changes his mind – and a leader who changes his policies – on a whim. Not too long ago, some Western leaders were hoping for a הֲפִיכָה (*hafikhah*), "coup d'état," in troublesome Iraq. Others would not be satisfied with anything less than a complete מַהְפֵּכָה (*mah'pekha*), "revolution."

Of course, there are still others who are willing לַהֲפֹךְ עוֹלָמוֹת (*la-hafokh olamot*), literally "to overturn worlds," figuratively "to move heaven and earth," even if it be the Jewish world and the Israeli heaven and earth, to find a peaceful solution to the problems of the Middle East. Are such people believers in magic? Let's hope not.

18

הרה

HEH, RESH, HEH

THE CONCEPTION OF A
NATION

You need only open today's newspaper to know that Jews have a fundamental need for connections – among themselves, between themselves and their land, and between their present and their past. And when you open a *mahzor*, a prayer book for the Days of Awe, you will find a phrase – הַיּוֹם הֲרַת עוֹלָם (*ha-yom harat olam*), "Today [Rosh Hashana, the Jewish New Year] the world was conceived" – that makes an organic connection between celebration and creation.

Jews also have a need to find connections between words. Take, for example, the root הרה (HEH, RESH, HEH), "to conceive." Astute readers will note a similarity of sound (often an excellent clue) between the words הוֹרֶה (*horeh*), "parent," and מוֹרֶה (*moreh*), "teacher." Would it not be elegant if there were an etymological connection between parents and teachers?

Unfortunately, the etymologist's fancy is bound by the history of the word. With even the best of will – unless you are one of those Jewish grammarians of the tenth century, like Menahem ben Saruk and Dunash ibn Labrat, who believed that all Hebrew roots were composed of two letters or even one letter – it is well nigh impossible to make a connection between the root ירה (YOD, RESH, HEH), from which מוֹרֶה (*moreh*) derives, and הרה (HEH, RESH, HEH), which is the source of הוֹרֶה (*horeh*).

There is no need to fret, however, for fanciful connections are available nevertheless. Does not the belly of a woman who is בְּהֵרָיוֹן (*be-herayon*), "pregnant," and who wears a שִׂמְלַת הֵרָיוֹן (*simlat herayon*), "maternity dress," resemble a mountain? Does not the Hebrew word for mountain, הַר (*har*), echo the first syllable of הָרָה (*harah*), "to conceive?" Although this connection may sound more farfetched than the one suggested earlier, there is a strong possibility that somewhere in our misty past הַר (*har*) and הָרָה (*harah*) are connected. Menahem and Dunash were not completely wrong, you know.

The verb הָרָה (*harah*) appears frequently in the Bible, more than twenty times in the formula וַתַּהַר וַתֵּלֶד (*va-tahar, va-teled*), "She conceived, she gave birth." Moses, whose claim to fame was his ability to connect very disparate human elements into a unified nation, uses our root to argue with God, a bit defensively perhaps, about his responsibility for the trespasses of his people: הֶאָנֹכִי הָרִיתִי אֵת כֹּל הָעָם הַזֶּה (*ha-anokhi hariti et kol ha-am ha-zeh*), "Was it I who conceived this nation?" (Numbers 11:12).

Today, the root is found most often in the plural noun הוֹרִים (*horim*), "parents." And in Israel, active parents can be found in their children's school as members of the Parent–Teacher Association, the וַעַד הַהוֹרִים (*va'ad ha-horim*).

One might say that, despite etymology, there will always be a connection, in the Jewish value system, between הוֹרִים (*horim*), parents, and מוֹרִים (*morim*), teachers.

19

זכר

ZAYIN, KHAF, RESH

YOU MUST REMEMBER THIS

If we judge by the number of times in the liturgy Rosh Hashana is also called יוֹם הַזִּכָּרוֹן (*yom ha-zikkaron*), the Day of Remembrance, we might conclude that remembering—by both God and man—is more central to the holiday than repentance.

It is not by accident that historian Yosef Haim Yerushalmi of Columbia University entitled his seminal book on Jewish historiography *Zakhor* (Seattle: University of Washington Press, 1982), "Remember," in the imperative. Yerushalmi argues that collective memory is such an important Jewish value that until the modern period many Jewish scholars had been willing to dispense with the formal writing of history in favor of remembering it through oral transmission and tradition.

The first two times that the root זכר (ZAYIN, KHAF, RESH), "to remember," appears in Scripture, God remembers that Noah is in an ark; He subsequently promises to remember into infinity the covenant He made with Noah after the Flood. That memory is an attribute of God can be deduced further from the name of the prophet Zechariah, which in Hebrew is זְכַרְיָה (*zekharyah*), "whom God remembers." One of the more poignant modern uses made of a classical phrase was articulated by David Ben-Gurion, who, eulogizing his late wife, Paula, at her funeral, quoted Jeremiah 2:2: זָכַרְתִּי לָךְ חֶסֶד נְעוּרַיִךְ (*zakharti lakh hesed ne'urayikh*), "I remember the affection of your youth."

In postbiblical Judaism, the root is used to show respect for both the Rabbis and God. One way to refer to the Rabbis of the Talmud is to call them חַז"ל (*hazal*), an acronym for חֲכָמֵינוּ זִכְרוֹנָם לִבְרָכָה (*hakhameinu zikhronam li-vrakhah*), "our Sages, may their memory be for a blessing." One way the Rabbis refer to the ineffable four-letter divine name is to call it the אַזְכָּרָה (*azkarah*), an Aramaic word that is also used to denote a memorial ceremony. Let us not forget the יִזְכֹּר (*yizkor*) service, which, according to social scientist Daniel Bell, ties Jews to the Jewish community. "In the *Yizkor,* through memory, I am identified as a Jew," says Bell.

Can a language be either pessimistic or optimistic? The forget-me-not, a flower that in English pleads negatively for love, is in Hebrew a זָכְרֵינִי (*zikhrini*), which asks one's beloved, in the most positive terms, to "remember me."

20

זמם

ZAYIN, MEM, MEM

AN ENTERPRISING PEOPLE

A society is often described by the character traits it most admires and the behaviors it rewards. There was a time when Westerners believed that the attribute most admired in Israeli society was חֻצְפָּה (*hutspah*), the brashness required to get things done.

Today, an observer of Israeli life will quickly conclude that the quality the modern Jewish state rewards is יָזְמָה (*yozmah*), "initiative." So pervasive is the appreciation of this feature that there are at least three synonyms in modern Hebrew for the enterprising someone who knows how to take initiative: a יָזְמָן (*yozman*), a יָזָּם (*yazzam*), and a בַּעַל יָזְמָה (*ba'al yozmah*). As Israel moves away from a socialist economy, two expressions, יָזְמָה חָפְשִׁית (*yozmah hofshit*), "free enterprise," and יָזְמָה פְּרָטִית (*yozmah peratit*), "private enterprise," are likely to become more common.

Curiously, both the classical source and the original root of this highly valued trait are pejorative in the extreme. The verb יָזְמוּ (*yazmu*) appears only once in Scripture, in connection with the builders of the Tower of Babel who, in Genesis 11:6, though they certainly took some initiative, nevertheless were condemned for plotting to do what the biblical narrative considers an evil deed.

According to most scholars, the root of this enigmatic verb is זמם (ZAYIN, MEM, MEM), a verb used in the Bible overwhelmingly in a negative sense. Deuteronomy 19:19 records that one of the most heinous of judicial crimes is that of עֵדִים זוֹמְמִים (*edim zomemim*), witnesses who conspire to pervert their testimony to convict an innocent person of a crime.

In the judgment of Rabbi Samson Raphael Hirsch, who wrote an etymologically based commentary on the Bible, the reprehensible quality attributable to these witnesses is that they exaggerated the obligation to bear witness and turned duty into a crime. Perhaps,

Hirsch suggests, the root of יָזַם (*yazam*), "He plotted," is the same as that for גָּזַם (*gazam*), "He exaggerated." Turning something ordinary into something extraordinary is not always negative. Witness the case of the Woman of Valor who זָמְמָה שָׂדֶה וַתִּקָּחֵהוּ (*zamemah sadeh va-tikahehu*), "proposed to acquire a field," and, says Hirsch, was able to purchase it by saving her ordinary pennies.

Speaking of valor, who do you suppose was the person credited with coining the modern word יָזְמָה (*yozmah*)? It was Eliezer Ben Yehuda himself, the enterprising man who took the initiative to reinvent the Hebrew language for modern living.

Was that a case of חֻצְפָּה (*hutspah*) or of יָזְמָה (*yozmah*)? Perhaps, in the final analysis, it was a little bit of both.

21

חבב

HET, VET, VET

LOVING AND OTHER DUTIES

If you walk along the streets of almost any city in Israel, sooner or later you're sure to hear someone exclaim יָה חֲבִּיבִּי (*yah habibi*). What he is *saying*, in Arabic, is something akin to "Oh, my beloved." What that person is *doing* is either trying to get someone's attention, using an expression similar to the English "You there," or showing affection by saying "Good to see you."

The old Semitic root from which this modern slang expression derives has taken some very interesting turns in biblical and rabbinic Hebrew. The root חבב (HET, VET, VET), "to love," occurs as a verb only once in Scripture, in Deuteronomy, in the expression חוֹבֵב עַמִּים (*hovev amim*), "He loves the nations." This verse has led to fervent dispute among the Rabbis. Does the root itself have a root? And would that root be חֹב (*hov*), "bosom," or חוֹב (*hov*), "indebtedness" or "duty"? Is someone loved because he is hidden, protected in a bosom, or is he loved because of duty? To compound the problem, and to offer a solution to it, we encounter another possible use of a biblical root in one of the names given to Jethro, the father-in-law of Moses, חוֹבָב (*hovav*). The Midrash says that Jethro, a Midianite priest, was called Hovav because he loved the Torah (and its duties) given by his son-in-law. Using this explanation, God loves the nations because He leads them to duty.

In modern Israel, the root has lost some of its intensity. Since אָהַב (*ahav*) serves nicely as the verb meaning "to love," חָבַב (*havav*) has taken on some of the connotations of "to like," as in הִיא מְחַבֶּבֶת אוֹתוֹ, אַךְ אֵינָהּ אוֹהֶבֶת אוֹתוֹ (*hi mehavevet oto, akh einah ohevet oto*), "She likes him but doesn't love him." One has to be cautious about using one of the more popular nouns derived from that verb. In modern Israeli slang, a חוֹבֶבֶת (*hovevet*) is a sexually active woman. For some reason, the masculine equivalent of this social type is not its lexical equivalent, חוֹבֵב (*hovev*). You'll find that noun in the Zionist expression חוֹבְבֵי צִיּוֹן (*hovevei tsiyon*),

---

"Lovers of Zion," and in חוֹבְבֵי שְׂפַת עֵבֶר (hovevei sefat ever), "lovers of the Hebrew language." Some communities express a great deal of חִבָּה (hibah), "esteem," for both types of lover, of Zion and of Hebrew. And while, in these communities, the last shall not always be first, the last is nevertheless special, as in the idiom using our root, אַחֲרוֹן אַחֲרוֹן חָבִיב (aharon aharon haviv), "last but not least."

Often, lovers of Hebrew are not only חוֹבְבִים (hovevim), "lovers," but also חוֹבְבָנִים (hovevanim), "hobbyists." Their תַּחְבִּיב (tahbiv), "hobby," involves reading, on a regular basis, about the roots and sources of Hebrew words. Sometimes, you'll even be able to hear one of them exclaim to a friend, "Yah habibi, did you see the outrageous things he wrote this time?"

22

חבל

HET, VET, LAMED

A WORD WITH A TWIST

Terrorism is a nasty word in any language. But חַבְּלָנוּת (*hablanut*), "sabotage," is a problem that Israelis (and Jews worldwide) have learned that they have to deal with. It is also a word that Israelis have learned to live with. Recently, an Israeli mother in a kibbutz playground — alluding to the behavior attributable to her son's "terrible twos" — referred to her little boy as הַחַבְּלָן שֶׁלִי (*ha-hablan sheli*). Of course, she didn't mean "my little terrorist" but was using the expression figuratively to describe her tyke's innocent mischief.

The root חבל (HET, VET, LAMED) has many figurative uses. Its original sense probably stems from a verb meaning "to twist" or from a noun that is a cognate of the English word "cable." The word חֶבֶל (*hevel*, accent on the first syllable) in Hebrew is a rope, something that must be twisted or braided into shape. These ropes must have been used originally on sailing ships, because the Hebrew word for sailor is חוֹבֵל (*hovel*), literally a "rope puller." On land, this rope was used as a measuring device for portions of real estate, hence the Hebrew word for "district," חֶבֶל (*hevel*), as in the erstwhile חֶבֶל עַזָּה (*hevel azah*), "Gaza District." In Hebrew, you don't throw out the baby with the bathwater, but sometimes you do inadvertently let the rope follow the bucket with similar results, as in הָלַךְ הַחֶבֶל אַחַר הַדְּלִי (*halakh ha-hevel ahar ha-deli*).

When things are tied into a bundle, you have a חֲבִילָה (*havilah*). A crafty strategy, with many twists, is a תַּחְבּוּלָה (*tahbulah*). The popular word for terrorism probably derives from the verb חָבַל (*haval*), to cause damage or injury.

When a rope is wound too tightly, it can cause a good deal of pain, hence the Hebrew word חֵבֶל (*hevel*), meaning "pain" or "pang." This word is used idiomatically in the plural to connote חֶבְלֵי לֵדָה (*hevlei ledah*), a woman's "birth pangs." More figuratively, it is found in the expression חֶבְלֵי מָשִׁיחַ (*hevlei mashiah*), "the birth pangs of the Messiah," the terrible suffering that the world is supposed to experience just prior to the arrival of the Messiah.

The root is used idiomatically – and frequently – in the exclamation חֲבָל (haval), "What a pity!" or "Too bad!" or, even more colloquially, "Tough!" The Rabbis, bemoaning the death of someone particularly cherished, would say חֲבָל עַל דְּאָבְדִין (haval al de-avdin), "Woe for such a loss." The word can also be found in the popular expression חֲבָל עַל הַזְּמָן (haval al ha-zeman), urging one's interlocutor to hurry up and put his time to good use.

One good use of time is to spend it learning Hebrew. Do so, and you'll never have to say חֲבָל (haval) about the way you have used *your* time.

23

חיה

HET, YOD, HEH

LIFE MEMBERSHIP

It is obvious to anyone who studies – or lives within – Judaism that life, חַיִּים (*hayyim*) – more than honor, beauty, or even *Shabbat* – is its central value.

The Torah emphasizes the primacy of the root חיה (HET, YOD, HEH), "to live," "to be vigorous." Arguably the most important tree in the Garden of Eden was the עֵץ הַחַיִּים (*ets ha-hayyim*), the "Tree of Life." The Torah explains that Eve was called חַוָּה (*havah*) because she was אֵם כָּל חַי (*em kol hai*), "the mother of all living beings." And when Joseph reveals himself to his brothers, he assuages their guilt for having sold him into slavery by reassuring them that God has sent him to Egypt for a reason: לְמִחְיָה (*le-mihyah*), to preserve life.

One of the most mystical names in Judaism comes from our root. Jewish lore teaches that one way to combat a life-threatening illness is to add the name חַיִּים (*hayyim*), "life," or חַיָה (*hayah*), "alive," to a sick person's name. This renaming ritual is based on the belief that names have both meaning and power.

The ordinary Jewish "man in the street" is often referred to in Yiddishized Hebrew as a חַיִּים־יַנְקל (*hayyim-yankl*). And speaking of Yiddish, let us not forget the expression for a refreshing pick-me-up, like a cool drink or a dip in the pool, אַ־מְחַיֶה (*a mekhayeh*).

In everyday Hebrew, an intensely lived experience is a חֲוָיָה (*havay-yah*), something you can promise to college students in your family to whom you suggest a trip to Israel. Since there is nothing more essential than life, it is not surprising that Hebrew should derive the word חִיּוּנִי (*hiyyuni*), "essential," from our root. So important is life that in Hebrew the popular expression for enjoyment is לַעֲשׂוֹת חַיִּים (*la-asot hayyim*), literally, "to make life." It would be superfluous in the extreme to remind our readers that the quintessential toast at Jewish life-cycle celebrations is לְחַיִּים (*le-hayyim*), "To life."

Life is not always rosy. Ask an Israeli how he or she is doing and you're likely to get the laconic answer חַיִּים (hayyim), "We're living." When things in the family aren't going too well economically, you might hear חַיִּים עַל בַּטָרִיּוֹת (hayyim al batareiot), "We're living on batteries," that is, on credit from the bank.

One of the more interesting creations of Eliezer Ben Yehuda, the man responsible for the תְּחִיָּה (tehiyyah), "rebirth," of modern Hebrew, is the scientific term for microbe, a חַיְדַּק (haidak), a thin living thing.

You will often hear the following two-word conversation on the street in Israel; בְּחַיֶּיךָ? בְּחַיַּי (— be-hayyekha? — be-hayyai), " — On your life? — I should live so." Jews, who are reluctant to swear oaths in God's name, will often think nothing of swearing on their own life, probably because they don't really mean it. Or perhaps, because we have a living language, we have learned to live with all its contradictions.

Is it a matter of pride or is it a matter of fact that the motto Jews have inscribed on the coat of arms they carry inside themselves is עַם יִשְׂרָאֵל חַי (am yisrael hai), "The nation of Israel lives"? Perhaps, in the final analysis, this slogan is a sign of the Jewish value system, which prizes life above all.

24

חכם

HET, KHAF, MEM

A WORD FOR THE WISE

Among the Four Sons of whom the Passover *Haggadah* speaks, Jewish parents recognize and identify with only one: the חָכָם (*hakham*), the Wise Son. What it means to be wise will differ from family to family. In the Maimonides family, for example, where little Moses grew up to be a philosopher, an ethicist, a physician, and a court Jew, the term חָכָם (*hakham*) was applied to four different types of people: there was the rationalist חָכָם (*hakham*), the moralist חָכָם (*hakham*), the skilled-artisan health professional חָכָם (*hakham*), and the politically astute חָכָם (*hakham*).

Other variations on the word חָכָם (*hakham*) can be found in both traditional Jewish sources and spoken Israeli Hebrew. For the Rabbis of the Talmud, wisdom was organically associated with the Land of Israel. They used to say אֲוִירָא דְּאֶרֶץ יִשְׂרָאֵל מַחְכִּים (*avira de-erets yisrael mahkim*), "The very air of the Land of Israel makes one wise." In answer to the question אֵיזֶהוּ חָכָם (*eizehu hakham*), "Who is wise?", the Rabbis of *Pirke Avot* used to answer, "One who learns from all people." Sefardic rabbinic leaders will often have the title of חָכָם (*hakham*), for example Hakham Rabbi Salomon Gaon, the late chair of Sefardic Studies at Yeshiva University. Talmudic Sages are also called חֲכָמִים (*hakhamim*), especially in the appellation חַזַ"ל (*hazal*), an abbreviation for חֲכָמֵינוּ זִכְרוֹנָם לִבְרָכָה (*hakhameinu zikhronam li-vrakhah*), "Our Sages, may their memory be for a blessing."

When passing from Babylonia to Eastern Europe, Jewish history makes a required stop at a certain *shtetl* where the חַכְמֵי חֶלֶם (*hokhmei helem*), the Wise Men of Chelm, were reputed to dwell. These men were "wise" according to what linguists call antiphrasis, that is to say, they were fools. Among the many benefits of having a sovereign state with a national language are a constantly developing vocabulary and a lack of self-consciousness about using it. All this is to say that modern

---

Israel has a variety of expressions for the designation "fool." Among them is חָכָם בַּלַּיְלָה (*hakham ba-lailah*), literally "a wise man at night," presumably because he runs a lesser risk of committing foolish acts when asleep.

The word חָכְמָה (*hokhmah*), "wisdom," used to be applied in Hebrew to the various sciences, for example, חָכְמַת הַטֶּבַע (*hokhmat ha-teva*), "natural sciences," or חָכְמַת הַחֶשְׁבּוֹן (*hokhmat ha-heshbon*), "mathematical sciences," both now obsolete. Today, it can be used to designate a field of academic study, like חָכְמָה יְוָנִית (*hokhmah yevanit*), Greek literature and philosophy, or חָכְמַת יִשְׂרָאֵל (*hokhmat yisrael*), Jewish Studies.

Interestingly, the plural of the word חָכְמָה (*hokhmah*) is used in Israel today with its Yiddish meaning of "the machinations of a wise guy" and is sometimes even spelled – and pronounced – not in the Hebrew חָכְמוֹת (*hokhmot*) but in the Yiddish חָכְמֶס (*hokhmes*).

Jewish wisdom asserts that שְׁאֵלַת חָכָם חֲצִי תְּשׁוּבָה (*she'elat hakham hatsi teshuvah*), "the question of the wise person constitutes half an answer." It would take a sophisticated parent, one who is מְתֻחְכָּם (*metukhkam*), or in the feminine מְתֻחְכֶּמֶת (*metuhkemet*), to work this discussion of the word חָכָם (*hakham*) into the question-and-answer part of the Seder. Not to worry. Jewish children recognize and identify with only one type of parent: one who has חָכְמָה (*hokhmah*).

25

חלץ

HET, LAMED, TSADI

THE PIONEERING SPIRIT

Like their American frontier counterparts, the early settlers of the *Yishuv* in *Erets Yisrael* – the חֲלוּצִים (*halutsim*), "pioneers" – had to travel great distances to arrive at the place of their settlement. Like the חֲלוּצִים (*halutsim*), words deriving from the root חלץ (HET, LAMED, TSADI) can be found all over the map of the Hebrew language.

This linguistic diversity stems no doubt from two seemingly contradictory meanings this root has in Scripture. At one pole the verb חָלַץ (*halats*) means to equip for war; at the other, the verb חִלֵּץ (*hilets*) means to rescue a soldier taken prisoner in battle.

The Book of Proverbs teaches that צַדִּיק מִצָּרָה נֶחֱלָץ (*tsaddik mi-tsarah nehelats*), "the righteous person is delivered out of trouble." This latter sense of removal was also used to describe the spoliation – the removal of the property – of a vanquished enemy. This idea of removal is also found in the biblical ceremony of חֲלִיצָה (*halitsah*), the removal of the sandal of a man who refuses to perform a levirate marriage with the childless widow of his dead brother or other close relative.

In modern Hebrew, the second meaning of the root, removal, can be found in the home of every Israeli oenophile. A חוֹלֵץ (*holets*), "corkscrew," is employed to remove the cork from a bottle of fine Israeli wine. (Even an earthy pioneer wouldn't want to drink wine from a bottle with a screw bottle cap.)

Is a חָלוּץ (*haluts*), therefore, someone who has uprooted himself, removed himself, from his home? It sounds good but is doubtful. Perhaps the archaic noun חֶלֶץ (*helets*), "loin," as in "to gird one's loins," is the key. After all, the hipbone juts out from the body, and just as the jutting hipbone leads the way as the body goes forward, so too does the pioneer lead the way for the body politic and social. It sounds doubtful but is probably correct.

A חֻלְצָה (*hultsah*), "blouse" or "shirt," is both a garment that is easily removed and a garment that covers the hips. A woman's children are called in classical Hebrew יוֹצְאֵי חֲלָצֶיהָ (*yotsei halatsehah*), the "issue of her loins."

On the *Shabbat* before the New Moon, we say a prayer asking for physical vigor, חִלּוּץ עֲצָמוֹת (*hiluts atsamot*), an action on the body's bones that could involve their strengthening or, for those who undertake a morning stretch, a loosening of the skeletal structure. On the subject of sports, a חָלוּץ (*haluts*) nowadays is not a pioneer but a forward on a soccer team.

The original חֲלוּצִים (*halutsim*) were in the vanguard of the Zionist movement. In the vanguard of these חֲלוּצִים (*halutsim*) was the Hebrew language, leading the way toward national cultural revival.

26

חסן

HET, SAMEKH, NUN

WHAT'S IN A MAGAZINE? EVERYTHING

When is a magazine more than simply a periodical? If you look up the word "magazine" in Joseph Shipley's *Dictionary of Word Origins* (Totowa, NJ: Littlefield, Adams, 1970), you'll learn that the word originally meant a storehouse and that in the eighteenth century, "magazine" was a frequent title of books that were intended as storehouses of information. Later on the word was applied to what we call periodicals, which, says Shipley, eventually "monopolized the term."

A look at the meaning of the French word *magasin*, "store," leads us to conclude that magazine and *magasin* are cognates, that is, they come from the same source. What does all this have to do with Hebrew? A look at – and the exaggerated pronunciation of – the Hebrew word מַחְסָן (*mahsan*), "warehouse," leads us to more than a conjecture that we are in the presence of that source. (The direct source may be that other Semitic language Arabic, but let's not quibble.)

The root of the word מַחְסָן (*mahsan*) is חסן (HET, SAMEKH, NUN), meaning "to store." In the Bible, the noun חֹסֶן (*hosen*) often means "riches," implying that what is stored up eventually becomes wealth. As one might expect, the word is found in proverbs that warn against relying on prosperity. After all, we are told, לֹא לְעוֹלָם חֹסֶן (*lo le-olam hosen*), "Wealth does not endure forever." Besides, בֵּית צַדִּיק חֹסֶן רָב (*bet tsaddik hosen rav*), "It is the house of a righteous person that is truly filled with riches."

In modern Hebrew, one can store up not only riches but also immunity, as in the expression for "inoculated" or "vaccinated," מְחֻסָּן (*mehusan*). A different type of immunity can be found in the diplomatic corps, where ambassadors have חֲסִינוּת דִּיפְּלוֹמָטִית (*hasinut diplomatit*), "diplomatic immunity." A third type of immunity relates to places and products, as in goods and warehouses that are חֲסִינֵי־אֵשׁ (hasinei-esh), "fireproof."

One of the earlist uses of the word "magazine" in English was in combination with the word "gunpowder." That sense is not absent from the Hebrew either. In a poem published not long ago in an Israeli magazine, a pizzeria owner returning to his shop in Tel Aviv from reserve duty in Gaza tells us פֵּרַקְתִּי אֶת הַמַּחְסָנִית (peirakti et ha-mahsanit), "I removed the magazine [filled with cartridges]," before sitting down to meditate on the long- and short-term problems caused by the *Intifada*. We learn a good deal about Israeli society's ability to confront its issues on the human level from the fact that this poem wound up in a magazine and not in the pizzeria's מַחְסָן (mahsan).

27

חתן

HET, TAV, NUN

HERE COMES THE GROOM

What is it about the month of June that turns speakers of English into speakers of Yiddish and, through Yiddish, into speakers of Hebrew as well? June is the month when everybody seems to be celebrating a *khassene*, a Jewish wedding. And, no matter whose side you're from, that's the time of the year you're always being introduced by your host or hostess to *mekhutonim*, in-laws of the bride or groom.

Both of these Yiddish words — it is obvious that they are Yiddish words from the transliterations — derive, of course, from the Hebrew root חתן (HET, TAV, NUN).

The origin of the root is a matter of some scholarly conjecture. Does it come from a legal term meaning to join the family of one's bride, to become an in-law? Or does it come from a verb meaning "to circumcise," a reference to a custom in many ancient civilizations in which the bridegroom was circumcised just prior to the wedding ceremony? (This conjecture might help to explain one of the more puzzling biblical stories dealing with Moses, in which we find the expression חֲתַן דָּמִים לַמּוּלֹת [*hatan damim lamulot*], "a bridegroom of blood for circumcisions.") One of the more appealing conjectures traces our root back to an Akkadian verb meaning "to protect." A חָתָן (*hatan*) would be someone who is protected by his wife's family.

In the biblical story of the destruction of Sodom, where we learn of Lot's futile attempt to save his חֲתָנִים (*hatanim*), "sons-in-law," that is the meaning of the word. We also learn how the lot of Moses is made easier by the suggestion made to him by יִתְרוֹ חֹתֵן מֹשֶׁה (*yitro hoten moshe*), "Yitro, the father-in-law of Moses," that he delegate some judicial authority to others. In this case, Jethro would be the protector of his son-in-law's sanity.

On Simhat Torah, the Festival of the Rejoicing of the Law, there are two חֲתָנִים (*hatanim*) in the synagogue, the חֲתַן תּוֹרָה (*hatan torah*) and the חֲתַן בְּרֵאשִׁית (*hatan bereshit*). These are the honorees called to the Torah for the last reading of the previous year's cycle and the first reading of the coming one. In modern Hebrew, the word חָתָן (*hatan*) is used to designate the recipient of any honor or prize, as in חֲתַן פְּרַס נוֹבֶּל (*hatan peras nobel*), "Nobel Prize winner."

Interesting information can be gathered by observing little children at play in the street. For some reason, Israeli popular culture prizes redheaded bridegrooms. How do we know? When two little girls say the same thing at the same time, one of them giggles and squeals יִהְיֶה לָךְ חָתָן ג'ינג'י (*yih'yeh lakh hatan dzhindzhi*), "You're going to have a redhead for a husband."

One person whose presence nobody prizes is a "wet blanket," that is, an אָבֵל בֵּין חֲתָנִים (*avel bein hatanim*), literally, "a mourner among bridegrooms." Surely better than that is someone who, in his or her determination to be joyous, always seems to try לִרְקֹד בִּשְׁתֵּי חֲתֻנּוֹת (*lirkod bishtei hatunot*), "to dance simultaneously at two weddings."

After all, isn't that what speakers of English who pepper their speech with Yiddish and Hebrew do?

28

טוס

TET, VAV, SAMEKH

FLIGHTS OF FANCY

Aside from all the other obvious advantages of flying to Israel on El Al, one major extra benefit accrues to lovers of Hebrew. By flying on El Al, those who enjoy musing about the roots and sources of Hebrew words can get immersed in their subject some ten hours earlier than they might otherwise do. Just thinking about the root for "to fly," for example, טוס (TET, VAV, SAMEKH), can keep you busy for hours.

The origin of this word, like that of many modern Hebrew words, is in the Bible. But there is a striking difference between the biblical and modern versions. The ancient Hebrew form in the Bible is טוש (TET, VAV, SIN). In the Book of Job we are reminded that our days fly by ever so swiftly, the way a vulture flies after food, כְּנֶשֶׁר יָטוּשׂ עֲלֵי אֹכֶל (ke-nesher yatus alei okhel). Curiously, this is the only place in the Bible where our word occurs in any form.

The Hebrew of our Rabbis already has our modern final SAMEKH (ס) in place of the original SIN (שׂ). (Of course, the pun *is* intended.) The Rabbis used the verb to describe not only mere physical flight but also the metaphorical hovering of the soul above the body.

In modern Israel, the root, like airplanes themselves, מְטוֹסִים (metosin), can be seen all over the landscape. Before you even get on the plane, you have to know the number of your flight, טִיסָה (tisa). That good-looking fellow in the cockpit, dressed in his snappy uniform, is the טַיָּס (tayas), "pilot." If you're lucky, maybe your marriageable daughter will fall in love with one of these, or with flying itself, called in Hebrew טַיִס (tayis, accent on the first syllable), and become a טַיֶּסֶת (tayeset), the feminine form for pilot, as well as the word for "squadron" (which no person, male or female, can become).

One of the catchiest Hebrew advertising slogans in recent memory was a play on our word: טַסְתִּי פַנְטַסְטִי עִם אֶל־עַל (tasti fantasti im el-al), "I had a fantastic flight with El Al."

Hebrew idioms, at least the ones that keep the language alive and vibrant, are often rooted in playfulness. In everyday speech, for example, a person who is a bit dizzy and sees things somewhat out of focus is called מְטֻשְׁטָשׁ (*metushtash*). Recalling that some letters are interchangeable, it did not take long for Israelis to see that by changing one letter — to form the word מְטֻשְׁטָס (*metushtas*) — one could coin a new word for a new phenomenon, "jet lag."

If you start your trip to Israel on El Al, you may still get the same jet lag as on any other airline — but you'll gain some Hebrew.

29

טעם

TET, AYIN, MEM

IN GOOD TASTE

There's no accounting for tastes, they say, whether you are choosing food or clothing, a spouse or an intellectual pursuit. Those obsessed with Hebrew derivations will no doubt agree that עַל טַעַם וָרֵיחַ אֵין לְהִתְוַכֵּחַ (al ta'am va-reiah ein le-hitvake'ah), "one does not debate taste and odor."

The root טעם (TET, AYIN, MEM) appears first in the biblical episode dealing with the rivalry between Jacob and Esau. To assure that it will be her son Jacob who will find favor in his father's eyes, our foremother Rebecca prepares for Isaac all sorts of מַטְעַמִּים (mat'ammim), "delicacies."

Tasting is what gets Jonathan into trouble with *his* father, King Saul. Not having heard a royal order to abstain from food, Jonathan confesses, טָעֹם טָעַמְתִּי מְעַט דְּבַשׁ (ta'om ta'amti me'at devash), "I had a taste of honey." He thus causes his father – not otherwise known for rational behavior – to lose control. King David only seems to lose control when he feigns madness to extricate himself from a difficult situation. He does it בְּשַׁנּוֹתוֹ אֶת טַעְמוֹ (be-shanoto et ta'amo), by changing not his sense of taste but his good sense, that is, by appearing to be insane.

Like many fundamental words in Jewish culture, our root often applies to making distinctions. That's what David means when, in Psalms, he prays טוּב טַעַם וָדַעַת לַמְּדֵנִי (tuv ta'am va-da'at lamdeni), "Teach me to have discernment." Anyone trained to chant the Torah learns to distinguish among the טַעֲמֵי הַמִּקְרָא (ta'amei ha-mikra), "cantillation signs."

Talmudic discourse requires both reason and reasons. The way to ask "What is the reason?" in Aramaic is מַאי טַעְמָא (mai ta'ama). Of a scholar adept in rabbinic casuistry, one says that he can find an impure animal pure בְּק"ן טְעָמִים (be-kan te'amim), "for one hundred fifty reasons." Causality is expressed in modern Hebrew in a prepositional phrase when, for example, we say of a friend that he returned early from vacation מִטַּעַם הַבְּרִיאוּת (*mi-ta'am ha-briut*), "for health reasons."

The most colorful use of the root, however, can be found on the pyramid-shaped packages of the Middle Eastern spice known as *za-'atar* (hyssop) sold in Israeli supermarkets. The packagers of this pungent herb took the expression "adds spice to your life," מוֹסִיף טַעַם לַחַיִּים (*mosif ta'am la-hayyim*), and turned it around to form an ingenious advertising slogan, מוֹסִיף חַיִּים לַטַּעַם (*mosif hayyim la-ta'am*), "adds life to your taste."

Whether spicy or bland, your taste is always good if you say it in Hebrew.

30

יד ה

YOD, DALET, HEH

JEWISH THANK TANK

Lord knows, there are many holidays celebrated in the modern State of Israel that were unknown to both the Israelites of the Torah and the Rabbis of the Talmud. The most glowing example of this phenomenon is, of course, Yom Ha-Atzma'ut, Israel Independence Day.

A much less familiar occurrence in Israel, celebrated by American *olim* come November, is called in Hebrew יוֹם הַהוֹדָיָה (*yom ha-hodayah*), "Thanksgiving Day." Look at the Hebrew word very carefully. Is it mere coincidence that the Hebrew word for the turkey that is at the center of the celebration is תַּרְנְגוֹל הֹדּוּ (*tarnegol hodu*)? To insinuate that a turkey might be a "chicken of thanks" is farfetched indeed. And yet, the real root for the courteous תּוֹדָה (*todah*), "thanks," strains one's credulity even further.

The *shoresh* in question is יד ה (YOD, DALET, HEH), containing within it the noun יָד (*yad*), "hand," and the verbal notion of throwing. How did יָדָה (*yadah*) come to mean "to acknowledge," "to agree," "to praise," "to thank"? Obviously, gestures sometimes accompany words to convey meaning. It is not too hard to visualize that a hand raised in a friendly manner would equal תּוֹדָה (*todah*), "thanks."

One of the most strained etymologies relating to our root comes from our foremother Leah, who asserts אוֹדֶה אֶת ה' (*odeh et ha-shem*), "I will thank God" by giving my fourth son the name יְהוּדָה (*yehudah*), implying that the name comes from our root. Who, in this context, is a Jew, a יְהוּדִי (*yehudi*)? One who thanks God. The Rabbis, of course, would have agreed. After all, the first prayer a Jew says upon arising is the מוֹדֶה אֲנִי (*modeh ani*), "I give thanks," and the only prayer in the daily *amida* that has two versions is the מוֹדִים (*modim*), "We give thanks."

In Israel today, a student who has not done his assignment might tell the teacher אֲנִי מוֹדֶה שֶׁלֹּא קָרָאתִי אֶת הַסֵּפֶר (*ani modeh she-lo karati et ha-sefer*), "I admit that I didn't read the book." Let's reward his honesty

---

with only a light punishment. After all, he did lead us to another deriv-ative of our root, וִדּוּי (vidui), "confession."

It's not exactly a confession, but our opening was not totally accu-rate. There are those who assert that Thanksgiving Day does have its source in the Torah. The Pilgrims, pious Bible readers that they were, adapted the biblical harvest festival of Sukkot to their needs and cre-ated a new holiday to thank God for His bounty. Thanks to them, הוֹדוֹת לָהֶם (hodot la-hem), we now have two reasons to say both תּוֹדָה (to-dah) and חַג שָׂמֵחַ (hag sameah).

31

יֶלֶד

YOD, LAMED, DALET

BOYS AND GIRLS TOGETHER

Jerusalem is a city for Jewish prophets and Jewish visionaries. When the prophets are not of the "gloom and doom" variety, Jerusalem is also a city for Jewish children.

It is uncanny how the prophet Zechariah's vision of Israel's ancient metropolis can be applied with Zionist panache to the capital city of the modern Jewish State. "Yet again," he proclaimed, "shall the streets of Jerusalem be filled with boys and girls – יְלָדִים וְילָדוֹת (*yeladim vi'ladot*) – playing."

It should not be surprising that the Hebrew words יֶלֶד (*yeled*), "boy," and יַלְדָה (*yaldah*), "girl," should have parturition – giving birth – at their source. The root ילד (YOD, LAMED, DALET) is found as a verb in countless biblical genealogies meaning just that, "to give birth." In English and the Romance languages it is the word "native" and its cognates that contain the sense of being born. Think of nativity and *naître* as but two prime examples. In Hebrew a native of Jerusalem is called a יְלִיד יְרוּשָׁלַיִם (*yelid yerushalayim*).

One of the most important statistics in Israel is the יְלוּדָה (*yeludah*), "birthrate." Two crucial professions for promoting what the Israelis like to call "interior *aliya*" are, despite the sexism inherent in their gender, the מְיַלֵד (*meyaled*), "obstetrician," and the מְיַלֶדֶת (*meyaledet*), "midwife."

The noun וָלָד (*valad*), when it means "embryo," can be heard and read in many contemporary discussions in modern Israel relating to the issue of abortion. The same noun also teaches us that in many cases the letters ו (VAV) and י (YOD) were at one time interchangeable. The Arab name Walid comes from a cousin to our root; it teaches us that the VAV was – and is today by Yemenite Jews – pronounced WAW. That, by the way, is how the letter is transliterated by the *Encyclopaedia Judaica*.

The word יַלְדָּה (*yaldah*) has an interesting twist to it. Officially, it is applied to girls only up to the age of nine. After that, a girl becomes a נַעֲרָה (*na'arah*) or a בַּחוּרָה (*bahurah*). Among themselves, Israeli women don't call themselves יְלָדוֹת (*yeladot*), "girls," but בָּנוֹת (*banot*), from the singular בַּת (*bat*), meaning "daughter."

Both יְלָדִים (*yeladim*) and יְלָדוֹת (*yeladot*) celebrate their birthdays, their יוֹם הֻלֶּדֶת (*yom huledet*), with great joy. Perhaps from their childish eagerness to have a party, the expression for birthday has been truncated into a single word, יוֹמוּלֶּדֶת (*yomuledet*), in everyday speech.

That's the way things go when you have a מוֹלֶדֶת (*moledet*), a "motherland," where Jewish boys and girls can play in a language of their own.

32

יסף

YOD, SAMEKH, FEH

ADDING BY ADDITION

Abba Eban, the most cosmopolitan of Israel's Laborites, was trying vainly to explain to his kibbutznik cronies back home that in golf it is the player with the *lower* score who wins. How could he make them understand this concept on their own terms? Eban was at an unaccustomed loss for words when he suddenly came up with an adage from the Talmud. In golf as in Jewish law, he exclaimed, כָּל הַמּוֹסִיף גּוֹרֵעַ (*kol ha-mosif gore'a*), "He who adds subtracts."

The root יסף (YOD, SAMEKH, FEH), meaning variously "to add," "to increase," "to do again," and "to continue," appears some two hundred times in Scripture, fully one-third of them with a negative connotation. For example, Joseph warns his brothers that if they do not return to Egypt accompanied by their baby brother Benjamin, לֹא תֹסִפוּן לִרְאוֹת פָּנָי (*lo tosifun lir'ot panai*), "You shall not see my face again."

The story of Joseph's name, יוֹסֵף (*yosef*), is interesting, to say the least. His mother, Rachel, calls him Yosef because she wants still *another* son, יֹסֵף...לִי בֵּן אַחֵר (*yosef . . . li ben aher*). We don't know how Yosef felt about being a mere pretext for a sibling, but we do know that in America some thousands of years later, the Bible-centered Mather family named their son "Increase" in English after the biblical hero Yosef. (Cotton Mather, Increase's son, got his name from the Hebrew word קָטָן [*katan*], "small.")

The Rabbis found the root most congenial. The rabbinic teachings that supplement the *mishnah* are called the תּוֹסֶפְתָּא (*tosefta*). The commentary on Rashi — Judaism's exegete par excellence — is called the תּוֹסָפוֹת (*tosafot*), the "additions"; the additional prayer recited on Sabbaths and holidays is called מוּסָף (*musaf*). The "Sunday" supplement to Israeli newspapers, appearing of course on Friday, is also called a מוּסָף (*musaf*).

In modern Hebrew the adjective מוּסָף (*musaf*) is found in the Israeli expression for the Value Added Tax, מַס עֶרֶךְ מוּסָף (*mas erekh musaf*), which taxes the value added to a product. To pay this and other taxes, Israelis often have to work overtime, שָׁעוֹת נוֹסָפוֹת (*sha'ot nosafot*). Luckily for the Israelis, however, when they go out to a restaurant, the price for the main course often includes two side dishes, תּוֹסָפוֹת (*tosafot*). The concert hall also provides free "additions"; the coda added at the end of a piece of music is called in Hebrew a יֵסֶף (*yesef*). And the addenda at the end of this book are called הוֹסָפוֹת (*hosafot*).

While it may be interesting to learn all these additions to our Hebrew vocabulary, we are enjoined by the Book of Ecclesiastes to take to heart that יוֹסִיף דַּעַת יוֹסִיף מַכְאוֹב (*yosif da'at yosif makh'ov*), "one who increases knowledge increases pain."

Let us hope that this warning does not apply to knowledge of Hebrew words.

33

יפה

YOD, FEH, HEH

BEAUTIFUL DREAMER

Hanukkah is a time when thoughtful Jews contemplate the meaning of the age-old conflict between Hebraism and Hellenism. Others, no less thoughtful, feel it more instructive to get to the "root" of the conflict by looking at the Hebrew word יָפֶה (*yafeh*), "beautiful."

Some would argue that the name of the third of Noah's sons, Japheth, יֶפֶת (*yefet*), derives from the root יפה (YOD, FEH, HEH). In rabbinic tradition, Japheth is credited with being the progenitor of יָוָן (*yavan*), Greece. In this way, beauty, associated with יֶפֶת (*yefet*), would be the source for the Greek concept of civilization.

Did the Rabbis really mean to exclude beauty from the sources of Judaism? It cannot be denied that in both religious and secular Jewish literature the root for beauty does have negative connotations. The author of the Book of Proverbs, describing the Woman of Valor, insists that הֶבֶל הַיֹּפִי (*hevel ha-yofi*), "Beauty is vanity." In modern times, Ahad Ha'am, the Zionist promoter of Jewish cultural rebirth, used the verb לְהִתְיַפּוֹת (*le-hityappot*), "to prettify," to describe Jews whose assimilationist proclivities led them to change their names and way of dress.

And yet, we do see beauty extolled in both biblical and rabbinic texts. This is the case, as might be expected, more than a dozen times in the Song of Songs. The beauty of the Bible's two greatest literary heroes, Joseph and David, is part of their heroic essence, the former described as יְפֵה תֹּאַר (*yefeh to'ar*), "of beautiful appearance," the latter as יְפֵה עֵינַיִם (*yefeh einayim*), "possessed of beautiful eyes." More surprisingly, perhaps, the Rabbis of the Talmud found it helpful in the pursuit of their didactic aims to insist that four biblical heroines—Sarah, Rahab, Abigail, and Esther—were more than merely "beautiful"; they were, in their own vocabulary, יְפֵהפִיּוֹת (*yefefiyot*), "extraordinarily beautiful."

In modern Israel, perhaps only a lawyer could explain how we

---

get from יִפּוּי (*yipui*), "embellishment," to יִפּוּי כֹּחַ (*yipui ko'ah*), "power of attorney." The adjective יָפֶה (*yafeh*) is often applied to the Land itself, especially when we speak of it as יְפֵה נוֹף (*yefeh nof*), "beautiful scenery." When applied to human actions, יָפֶה (*yafeh*) also has the connotation of "pleasantness," as in the negative expression זֶה לֹא יָפֶה מִצִּדְךָ (*zeh lo yafeh mi-tsidkha*), "It's not nice of you to do that."

In Israel, you'll see the noun יוֹפִי (*yofi*) on signs indicating that you're in front of a מָכוֹן יוֹפִי (*makhon yofi*), "beauty salon." As an exclamation in colloquial speech, the word יוֹפִי (*yofi*) has the same meaning as the English "Great!" The nonsense rhyme יוֹפִי טוֹפִי (*yofi tofi*) used to be found with some frequency as the Hebrew equivalent of "Outtasight!" but this idiom is being replaced by שִׁגָּעוֹן (*shiga'on*), "Crazy!"

The most tortured use of the root today is to be found in the expression יְפֵה נֶפֶשׁ (*yefeh nefesh*), "beauty of soul." Originally, this term was applied to gentle people. Now it is used acerbically in what sometimes passes for Israeli political discourse to describe a "left-wing-bleeding-heart-liberal-who-is-in-favor-of-giving-back-the-territories."

The way Israeli Jews react to the beauty in their tradition will determine whether Israel will become the מְדִינָה לְמוֹפֵת (*medinah le-mofet*), "model state," that Ahad Ha'am envisioned. If, as some think, the word מוֹפֵת (*mofet*) is derived from יָפֶה (*yafeh*) — models are usually beautiful — we need only sprinkle our conversations with the positive uses of our root to lead toward this desired end.

34

יצא

YOD, TSADI, ALEF

METAPHOR & *MOTSI*

One of the distinguishing marks of the Jewish people is the constant effort to turn the ordinary into the extraordinary.

Take the mundane act of eating a piece of bread, which we sanctify by reciting the blessing הַמּוֹצִיא לֶחֶם מִן הָאָרֶץ (*ha-motsi lehem min ha-arets*), "Who brings forth bread from the earth." What is truly extraordinary here is that in making this blessing and listening to what it says, we bypass the ordinary human tasks of planting, harvesting, milling, and baking and speak in supernatural metaphors of "bread-from-the-earth." We then take the verb, turn it into a noun, and make it the name for the blessing itself — as in "Recite the *Motsi*."

So useful is the ordinary Hebrew verb יָצָא (*yatsa*), "to go out," that it is found in dozens of expressions where imagery is at a remove from prosaic meaning. The root appears over a thousand times in Scripture. What is a soldier in the Bible but a יוֹצֵא צָבָא (*yotse tsava*), one who "goes out" to the army? And what are offspring but צֶאֱצָאִים (*tse'et-sa'im*), those who "come out" of their parents?

One of the more beautiful ethical injunctions of the Torah, using yet another form of the root, is מוֹצָא שְׂפָתֶיךָ תִּשְׁמֹר (*motsa sefatekha tish-mor*), literally, "Observe that which comes out of your mouth," figuratively, "Fulfill your promises."

Interestingly, the form מוֹצָא (*motsa*) is found in other contexts as well: in the expression מוֹצָאֵי שַׁבָּת (*motsa'ei shabbat*), Saturday night; in the name of the town Motsa, observed as you "exit" Jerusalem; and in the expression used to designate someone's ancestry, for example in מִמּוֹצָא סְפָרַדִי (*mi-motsa sefaradi*), "of Sefardic origin."

Sometimes an idiom based on the verb develops both religious and secular usages. In the Song of Songs the Daughters of Zion are urged צְאֶינָה וּרְאֶינָה (*tse'ena u-re'ena*), "Go out and see." From that admonition we get the name of the popular Yiddish translation of the

Torah and commentaries destined for women, the *Tsenarena*, as well as the title of Israel's most popular *horah*, "*Tzena, Tzena*."

In modern Israel, the root is found in ordinary social situations: as you observe your friend who has lost his cool, יָצָא מִכֵּלָיו (*yatsa mikelav*), literally, "went out of his instruments"; as you listen to the sports results, תּוֹצָאוֹת (*totsa'ot*) "results"; or, in your budget, as you tally up your הוֹצָאוֹת (*hotsa'ot*), "expenses." An exporter of Israeli products is a יְצוּאָן (*yetsu'an*) while the person who brings writers' words to light is a מוֹצִיא לָאוֹר (*motsi la-or*), "publisher."

What makes all of this ordinariness extraordinary, יוֹצֵא מִן הַכְּלָל (*yotse min ha-kelal*), is that it is said in Hebrew, an exceptional language on many counts.

35

ירה

YOD, RESH, HEH

TEACH ME TONIGHT

It is always appropriate, always timely, to pay homage to the Jewish community's most influential natural resource, its מוֹרִים (*morim*) and מוֹרוֹת (*morot*), "teachers."

The root of the noun מוֹרֶה (*moreh*) teaches us a great deal about how the Hebrew language works. Originally, the verb יָרָה (*yarah*) meant "to shoot," "to throw," "to cast," as in the phrase יָרָה חֵץ (*yarah hets*), "He shot an arrow."

Since early speakers of Hebrew saw rain as the "throwing" of water from Heaven, they called the rain at the beginning of the rainy season in Israel the יוֹרֶה (*yoreh*). Of the two types of rabbinic ordination, the one that certifies that the candidate can teach is called יוֹרֶה יוֹרֶה (*yoreh yoreh*). To get from the delivery of rain to the delivery of knowledge, one admittedly has to pass through a field of metaphors. But that's exactly how the Hebrew language progresses, through the imagination of its speakers.

To say that the verb יָרָה (*yarah*) is found in the Torah is to enunciate a play on words. After all, the root of תּוֹרָה (*torah*) is ירה (YOD, RESH, HEH). How do we know that the תּוֹרָה (*torah*) is a teaching text? In Exodus 4:15, Moses and Aaron are told, וְהוֹרֵיתִי אֶתְכֶם אֵת אֲשֶׁר תַּעֲשׂוּן (*ve-horeiti etkhem et asher ta'asun*), "I shall teach you what you shall do." Torah, in this context, does not mean the "Law" but "instruction." And God, in the same context, would be a teacher.

In the expression תּוֹרַת אִמֶּךָ (*torat immekha*), found in the famous "Letter of the Ramban to His Son," the word *torah* is applied to "your mother's teaching." In modern Hebrew, תּוֹרָה (*torah*) also has a secular use, as, for example, when speaking of תּוֹרַת הַמְּדִינָה (*torat ha-medinah*), "political science," or תּוֹרַת הַיַּחֲסוּת (*torat ha-yahasut*), Einstein's "theory of relativity."

The noun מוֹרֶה (*moreh*) does not mean only teacher. When you go touring in Israel, the person who meets you at your hotel in the morning to take you on a tour is your מוֹרֶה דֶרֶךְ (*moreh derekh*), your "tour guide." When rabbis and other Jewish scholars talk about "The *Moreh*," they are not referring to a person at all but to a book, Maimonides' *Guide for the Perplexed*, the מוֹרֶה נְבוּכִים (*moreh nevukhim*). That the term מוֹרֶה (*moreh*) is a term of honor can be seen from the expression מוֹרַי וְרַבּוֹתַי (*morai ve-rabotai*), the Hebrew equivalent of "ladies and gentlemen." It is also evident from the expression that one is supposed to use when addressing one's parents: אָבִי מוֹרִי (*avi mori*) and אִמִּי מוֹרָתִי (*immi morati*), "my parent, my teacher." One might ask whether there is a linguistic connection between a מוֹרֶה (*moreh*), "teacher," and a הוֹרֶה (*horeh*), "parent." If you read chapter 18 carefully, you already know the answer to that question.

36

כבש

KHAF, VET, SHIN

THE CONQUEST OF
THE ... PICKLE?

Sometimes, the way a language develops poses more questions than it answers. What are we to make, for example, of the fact that the same Hebrew root, כבש (KHAF, VET, SHIN), has generated meanings as diverse as "road," "conquest," "mystery," and, of all things, "pickling"? Is this diversity meant to teach us something about Jewish history? Jewish values? Judaism?

In the Torah, the verb כָּבַשׁ (kavash) has the primary meaning of "to dominate" or "subdue." This is evident in the first recorded mitsvah, which enjoins human beings not only to "be fruitful, multiply, and fill the earth" but also וְכִבְשֻׁהָ (ve-khivshuhah), in the imperative, "Subdue it."

Even to appear to subjugate a human being has disastrous consequences in the Bible. In the Book of Esther, the king, finding Haman seated on the queen's bed, cries out angrily, הֲגַם לִכְבּוֹשׁ אֶת הַמַּלְכָּה עִמִּי בַּבָּיִת (hagam likhbosh et ha-malkah imi ba-bayit?), "Would you violate the queen in my very presence?"

In rabbinic literature, the verb takes on a sense of moral conquest, as in the saying in *Pirke Avot,* אֵיזֶהוּ גִבּוֹר הַכּוֹבֵשׁ אֶת יִצְרוֹ (eizehu gibbor, ha-kovesh et yitsro), "Who is a hero? One who conquers his [evil] inclination." The Rabbis also tell a charming *midrash* about forefather Abraham who, because he destroyed his father's idols, was thrown into a כִּבְשָׁן אֵשׁ (kivshan esh), a "fiery furnace," by Nimrod, only to be rescued by the angel Gabriel. In this context, our root signifies reduction, as in reduction to ashes.

From our root we also learn that the ancients had a method of preserving vegetables that involved squeezing the liquid out. This process gave rise to Hebrew terms for canned vegetables כְּבָשִׁים (kevashim) and pickled products כַּבֶּשֶׁת (kabeshet). For the Rabbis, כְּבָשִׁים (keva-

shim) are also hidden things. A prophet may seek לִכְבֹּשׁ אֶת נְבוּאָתוֹ (*likh-vosh et nevuato*), "to suppress his prophecy," to hide it.

The ability of Hebrew to adapt venerable roots to modern needs is evident in the ancient Hebrew word for road, כְּבִישׁ (*kevish*). How is a road constructed? By compacting the earth, by pressing it down. Later on, when asphalt was added, it was necessary to invent the מַכְבֵּשׁ כְּבִישִׁים (*makhbesh kevishim*), "steamroller."

We learn from all this that you can't suppress a good nation for long. Or, as they say in fancy Hebrew, כָּל דָּבָר שֶׁהוּא נִכְבָּשׁ סוֹפוֹ לָצוּף (*kol davar shehu nikhbash sofo latsuf*), "Whatever is pressed down – oppressed or suppressed – always floats back to the top."

37

כון

KHAF, VAV, NUN

PREPARATION + INTENTION = MACHINATION

Which is more important, good intentions or positive results? It is certainly rare in Jewish or Zionist circles to find an apologist for fruitless good intentions. It is much more likely that you will hear someone making the case for positive results, even when achieved without כַּוָּנָה (kavvanah), "intent."

Even here, however, the issue is fuzzy. Take, for example, the Passover Seder. Is it enough to savor the four prescribed cups of wine as you might do at your local bistro? Obviously not. The Rabbis insisted on intention. They were careful to insert into the *Haggadah* the formula הִנְנִי מוּכָן (hineni mukhan), "Behold I am prepared" to drink the prescribed cup and thereby to perform a *mitsvah*.

Both כַּוָּנָה (kavvanah), "intention," and הֲכָנָה (hakhanah), "preparation," stem from the three-letter root כון (KHAF, VAV, NUN). Illustrative of the difference between the two branches stemming from this root are two verbs in the reflexive mode: לְהִתְכַּוֵּן (le-hitkavven), "to intend," "to mean," and לְהִתְכּוֹנֵן (le-hitkonen), "to get oneself ready."

In the first case, there is a sense of setting things straight, of aligning. An analogy with music may be helpful. Before the concert begins, it is important to make sure that הַכִּנּוֹר מְכֻוָּן (ha-kinnor mekhuvvan), "the violin is in tune." Sometimes, the musician does it himself. Sometimes a specialist, for example, a כַּוָּן פְּסַנְתֵּרִים (kavvan pesanterim), a "piano tuner," is called in.

In civilian life, no less than in the army, good sense requires us לְכַוֵּן אֶת הַשְּׁעוֹנִים (le-khaven et ha-sheonim), "to synchronize our watches." Before the soldier shoots his rifle, he takes aim by looking through his weapon's כַּוֶּנֶת (kavvenet), "sight." And how many times, when asking the way, have you been told that you're heading in the wrong כִּוּוּן (*kivvun*), "direction"?

The second sense of כון (KHAF, VAV, NUN) has to do not with setting things straight but with setting things up, preparing, instituting. The preparatory class in a Jewish school is a מְכִינָה (*mekhinah*). A machine institutes what a human intends. The Latin word *machina* and the Hebrew מְכוֹנָה (*mekhonah*), "machine," are related. Before the computer revolution, someone who intended to write a Hebrew language column for English speakers would compose his text on a מְכוֹנַת כְּתִיבָה (*mekhonat ketivah*), a "typewriter."

There are some people who live off what others have prepared, or, as they say in Hebrew, חַיִּים מִן הַמּוּכָן (*hayyim min ha-mukhan*). Others "institute" things for themselves, and that's how we get the Hebrew word מָכוֹן (*makhon*), "institute," for example, the מְכוֹן וַיצְמַן (*mekhon veitsman*), the Weizman Institute of Science, in Rehovot, Israel, or the מְכוֹן יוֹפִי (*mekhon yofi*), the "beauty parlor" down the street in Tel Aviv.

Both are practical places, and both have good intentions.

38

כלה

KHAF, LAMED, HEH

CULMINATIONS

Sooner or later, people who study the origins of words will start asking themselves ultimate questions. Why, for example, was language given to humans? One answer sounds suspiciously cynical at first glance: language was given to humans so that they might better hide what they really think.

Some people, not at all cynically, consider that use of language to be at the core of civility. The root כלה (KHAF, LAMED, HEH), with its multiple uses at weddings, conferences, crownings, and completions, is instructive in this matter.

In Judaism, polite speech often goes together with correct behavior. The Rabbis of the Talmud teach us that it is appropriate when greeting a bride, for example, to say, כַּלָּה נָאָה וַחֲסוּדָה (kallah na'ah va-hasudah), "What a beautiful and charming bride." This formula is in place, they insisted, because the *mitsvah* of לְשַׂמֵּחַ חָתָן וְכַלָּה (le-same'ah ha-tan ve-kallah), "making the bride and groom joyful," takes precedence over any obligation to be objective or truthful.

The verb כָּלָה (kalah) in one of its streams means "to be completed." Thus at the beginning of the New Year, we say hopefully, תִּכְלֶה שָׁנָה וְקִלְלוֹתֶיהָ (tikhleh shanah ve-kilelotehah), "May the old year end, with all its maledictions." The *Adon Olam* prayer sung at the end of the *Shabbat* services proclaims that אַחֲרֵי כִּכְלוֹת הַכֹּל (aharei kikhlot hakol), "even after the end of the everything," God will still reign. Note that in both of these examples "completion" contains the nuance of "destruction."

The word כַּלָּה (kallah), "bride," appears in Scripture with several nuances. The Book of Jeremiah repeats the phrase קוֹל חָתָן וְקוֹל כַּלָּה (kol hatan ve-kol kallah), "the voice of the groom and the voice of the bride," several times. From those four words the Jewish people have deduced that we're supposed to sing with gusto at Jewish weddings, especially the song with those words as the refrain. In the Book of Ruth we

---

get another meaning of the word כַּלָּה (*kallah*); there it refers not to a bride but to Naomi's daughters-in-law, Ruth and Orpah. The Song of Songs, for its part, adds another meaning. The sense of the expression אֲחוֹתִי כַלָּה (*ahoti kallah*), literally "my sister-bride," is somewhat closer to "my beloved."

Among the mystics of Safed a כַּלָּה (*kallah*) is God's betrothed, the Sabbath. Their practice was to go out and greet the "Sabbath bride" every Friday evening singing לְכָה דוֹדִי לִקְרַאת כַּלָּה (*lekhah dodi likrat kallah*), "Go, my beloved, to greet the bride." In a completely different rabbinic context, a כַּלָּה (*kallah*) is a large conference of adult students. These groups convened at Babylonian *yeshivot* during the vacation periods of the months of Adar and Elul, known as the יַרְחֵי כַּלָּה (*yarhei kallah*), "the months of completion."

How do we get from a bride to a seminar? The development of a group of Hebrew words having to do with culminations provides a clue. It appears that in ancient times a bride would wear a כְּלִיל (*kelil*), "crown," on her head. The noun כְּלִילוּת (*kelilut*), "nuptials," and the verb הִכְלִיל (*hikhlil*), "to wed"—both having to do with the "crowning" of the bride—are related to the adjective כָּלִיל (*kalil*), used to describe a "culmination in perfection." Further, there is another verb, כָּלָה (*kalah*), to "fulfill ideally."

There was a time when it was universally agreed in Judaism that the way for a young girl to fulfill herself was to become a כַּלָּה (*kallah*), a "bride," the way a *kallah* in a *yeshivah* was the culmination and fulfillment of the academic session. Whatever other issues they may cause to arise, both meanings of כַּלָּה (*kallah*) assure some measure of תַּכְלִית (*takhlit*), or, in its Yiddish derivative, *takhles*, not only purpose but also achievement.

39
כלי

KHAF, LAMED, YOD
INSTRUMENTALITY

In America, people take foreign languages casually; we are content to get a foreign word or expression *almost* right.

An article appearing not too long ago in the *New York Times Magazine* tells us for example that *klezmer* is a Yiddish word meaning "vessel of music." That is not its Yiddish meaning but its Hebrew origin. More precisely, the Yiddish noun *klezmer* means "popular musician"; in Hebrew, כְּלֵי זֶמֶר (*kelei zemer*) is a plural expression meaning "musical instruments."

The word כְּלִי (*keli*) appears 324 times in Scripture. Often the word כֵּלִים (*kelim*) is used when you don't want to be precise about its meaning; it refers to indeterminate "things." There is a whole tractate of the Mishna that bears the name כֵּלִים (*kelim*). It deals with vessels, to be sure, but also with laws pertaining to clothing, furniture, weapons, and all kinds of implements.

The biblical injunction against cross-dressing tells us that a man shall not wear a כְּלִי אִשָּׁה (*keli ishah*), a "dress." And while this usage was taken literally by the Rabbis, other words underwent metaphorical transformations. Thus, in the war-torn Book of Samuel, an "arms bearer" was called a נוֹשֵׂא כֵלִים (*noseh kelim*). In more peaceful times, the expression is used for a leader's "right-hand man." In a poetic move, medieval rabbis — whose only battles were textual — took the expression and applied it to the commentaries. Thus Rashi and Tosafot were called the נוֹשְׂאֵי כֵּלִים (*nos'ei kelim*) of the Talmud. Similarly, a distinguished personage is called a כְּלִי יָקָר (*keli yakar*), literally, a "dear vessel."

The holy vessels of the Temple were called the כְּלֵי קֹדֶשׁ (*kelei kodesh*). While the Temple is no more and we no longer have its ritual instruments (except in museums of the hopeful), the expression כְּלֵי קֹדֶשׁ (*kelei kodesh*) survives in the religious vocabulary. Today, those who toil for the community — the rabbi, the cantor, the *shamash*, the *gabbai*, and the members of the *Hevrah Kadisha* — are our כְּלֵי קֹדֶשׁ (*kelei kodesh*), "instruments of holiness." For some reason, the last of these — the members of the burial society — often have an unassuming character. In Hebrew, one says of an unpretentious person that he is נֶחְבָּא אֶל הַכֵּלִים (*nehba el ha-kelim*), "hidden among the instruments."

In Israel today, you'll hear the word כֵּלִים (*kelim*) used in connection with the daily ritual of washing the dishes. More than once a parent — or spouse — has been known לָצֵאת מִכֵּלָיו (*la-tset mi-kelav*), "to lose one's temper," over that issue. We would be wiser to save our temper tantrums for the misuses of language.

40

כנס

KHAF, NUN, SAMEKH

JEWISH TOGETHERNESS

As the Preacher in the Book of Kohelet reminds us, "For every thing there is a season." Among the most curious of these seasons is עֵת כְּנוֹס אֲבָנִים (*et kenos avanim*), "the season for gathering stones." The *Jerusalem Post*'s "Dry Bones" cartoonist Yaakov Kirschen would probably suggest that *that* season is *erev Shabbat* in the Ramot section of Jerusalem, the scene some time ago of some disruptive stone-throwing in the name of Judaism. Whatever Kohelet had in mind, however, the root כנס (KHAF, NUN, SAMEKH) is used in Hebrew at all times of the year.

The most common sense of the word today is "to gather." If there is anything that characterizes the Jewish people, it is that they negotiate historical milestones collectively. Queen Esther, in the face of communal disaster, sent out the word: לֵךְ כְּנוֹס אֶת כָּל הַיְּהוּדִים (*lekh kenos et kol ha-yehudim*), "Go gather all the Jews." The prayer for the ingathering of the Jews in Israel is found in the liturgical entreaty, וּנְפוּצוֹתֵינוּ כַּנֵּס (*u-nefutsoteinu kanes*), "Gather our dispersed."

There are several nouns for gathering, the most prominent being the כְּנֶסֶת (*kenesset*), the Parliament of Israel, the Knesset; the בֵּית כְּנֶסֶת (*beit kenesset*), the "synagogue" where Jews gather for prayer; and the כְּנֵסִיָּה (*keneissiyyah*), the "church" where Christians gather for similar purposes. In Jewish communal life, everybody gathers – not only politicians and religious people. Scholars and laypeople gather at their organizations' annual conferences. So frequent is this activity that there are even two words in Hebrew for the same activity: כֶּנֶס (*kenes*) and כִּנּוּס (*kinus*).

Another related meaning of the root is "to enter," from the verb נִכְנַס (*nikhnas*). The entrance of a building is a כְּנִיסָה (*kenissah*). To help a bride financially to enter into the covenant of marriage is called הַכְנָסַת כַּלָּה (*hakhnassat kallah*). Nobody is certain when and where the first pair of pants was invented, but it was probably much earlier than sixteenth-century Italy, when the comic theatrical character Pantale-one strutted the stage in his outlandish "pantaloons." What we do know is that the garment into which Israelite priests put their legs was called מִכְנָסַיִם (*mikhnasayim*), literally, "a pair of enterings." Today, in any Tel Aviv boutique, that's how you ask for a pair of trousers.

Solomon, the author of Kohelet, was not the only wise person to use our root. The Rabbis were also keen observers of humanity, and they used to say, נִכְנַס יַיִן יָצָא סוֹד (*nikhnas yayin yatsa sod*), "When wine goes in, secrets come out." Secrets also come out of words that are looked at with care.

41

כפר

KHAF, FEH, RESH

COVER–UP DAY

You can't open your newspaper these days without shaking your head in dismay over yet another story of an often pathetic attempt to engage in a cover-up of scandalous behavior.

Curiously, every fall, without so much as a by-your-leave, Jews the world over engage in a ritual cover-up of their improprieties of the past year. They call it Yom Kippur.

The Hebrew root כפר (KHAF, FEH, RESH), from which we get כִּפּוּר (*kippur*), first occurs in the Bible in God's instructions to Noah concerning the building of the ark. The shipbuilder is told to cover his vessel inside and out with pitch. The Hebrew word for the verb "to cover" here is כָּפַר (*khafar*); the one for the pitch covering is כֹּפֶר (*kofer*).

The Torah abounds in a variety of similar derivatives. The crusty frozen dew that covers the ground on a cold morning is called כְּפוֹר (*kefor*), "hoarfrost"; the word used to designate the cover of the holy ark is כַּפּוֹרֶת (*kaporet*); and the very rare word for a drinking vessel, כְּפוֹר (*kefor*), gets its name from the fact that it was plated with a protective covering.

Rabbi Samson Raphael Hirsch, in his commentary on Leviticus, tells us that to engage in כַּפָּרָה (*kapparah*) "literally is to 'cover' us from the effects of a sinful past." It does not take too much imagination to see how יוֹם הַכִּפּוּרִים (*yom ha-kippurim*), the Day of Atonement, should have started out as a day of cover-up. An effective way to pacify God would be to conceal one's sins. Of course, the best way to do that would be to atone for them, the cover-up becoming a protective white-wash, so to speak.

It takes a great deal more imagination to see how the word כַּפָּרָה (*kapparah*) came to mean a chicken. Of course it means that only when a fowl is waved over the head in the Erev Yom Kippur ritual known in Yiddish as *shlogn kapores*.

Two words stemming from our root have tried the ingenuity of

Hebrew etymologists. What are we going to do, after all, with כְּפָר (*ke-far*), "village," and כְּפִיר (*kefir*), "young lion"? Are we going to say that the כְּפִיר (*kefir*) has just begun to grow the hair — that is, the head covering — that older lions are famous for? And that what distinguishes a כְּפָר (*kefar*) from a field is that when you live in a village you have a roof covering your head? And what about the word כֹּפֶר (*kofer*), "ransom"? At least here we are redeeming a life, the object of כַּפָּרָה (*kapparah*).

If you think that this discussion has come far from the notion of cover-up, we can return to it via the notion of כְּפִירָה (*kefirah*), "heresy." Just as Noah's ark is blackened with tar, so too is the soul blackened when one denies the oneness of the Jewish God. Of course, on Yom Kippur we don't like to talk about such things. We cover them up.

42
כֹּשֶׁר

KHAF, SHIN, RESH
FITNESS, JEWISH STYLE

It is not unheard of for the word "kosher" to appear in your local Jewish newspaper or national magazine as many as twenty-five times in an issue, especially during the Passover season.

While the word "kosher" in "Kosher for Passover" is perfectly acceptable English usage, it is not exactly so in Hebrew. The English word "kosher" derives most probably from a Yiddish word, rhyming with *usher*, that was transliterated as *kosher*, the short ŏ of the Yiddish eventually becoming a long ō in English. A traditional Passover greeting in Yiddish is *"Hot mir a kosheren pesakh, mit gute kneidlakh."* (If you need a translation or help with the pronunciation, go on to the next paragraph, where the Hebrew part of this chapter properly begins.)

The Hebrew word כֹּשֶׁר (*kosher*, accent on the first syllable) is not the adjective describing ritually appropriate food that we're all familiar with – *that* word is כָּשֵׁר (*kasher*, accent on the second syllable) – but a noun meaning "fitness," "faculty," or "capability." The noun כֹּשֶׁר (*kosher*) is found in such expressions as כֹּשֶׁר רְאִיָּה (*kosher re'iyah*), the "faculty of sight," כֹּשֶׁר גוּפָנִי (*kosher gufani*), "physical fitness," and כֹּשֶׁר עֲלִיָּה (*kosher aliyah*), which has nothing to do with taking two sets of dishes when you go to settle in Israel but refers to the capability of heavy trucks and buses to climb Israel's steep hills.

The adjective כָּשֵׁר (*kasher*, the French – ever so precise in their pronunciation – often spell it *cachère*) is not applied solely to ritually prepared food. If Diogenes had looked among the Jews, he would not have needed a lantern in his search for an honest man. He would have found an אָדָם כָּשֵׁר (*adam kasher*), an "honest man," in the vocabulary of Jewish life.

Every plane in the El Al fleet may serve kosher food but, more importantly, it also has to be כָּשֵׁר לְטִיסָה (*kasher le-tissah*), "airworthy." And while not all food is כָּשֵׁר (*kasher*), you will certainly recognize the following proverb, found in the wisdom of all nations, הַכֹּל כָּשֵׁר בְּאַהֲבָה וּבְמִלְחָמָה (ha-kol kasher be-ahavah u-ve milhamah), "All's fair in love and war."

The root כשר (KHAF, SHIN, RESH) forms the basis of one of the most important nouns in the Zionist vocabulary, הַכְשָׁרָה (hakhsharah), "preparation," used in Zionist youth movements to describe the period of training prior to aliyah. Bnei Akiva, for example, has a summer trip to Israel for teenagers called, in their inimitable way, *Mach Hach*, more properly מַחֲנֵה הַכְשָׁרָה (mahaneh hakhsharah), "preparatory camp." The Jewish National Fund uses the word הַכְשָׁרָה (hakhsharah) to describe one of its main functions, the preparation of land for habitation.

You certainly have the כִּשּׁוּרִים (kishurim), "qualifications," and כִּשָּׁרוֹן (kisharon), "talent," not only to have a חַג כָּשֵׁר וְשָׂמֵחַ (hag kasher ve-sameah), "a kosher and happy holiday," but when the time comes, also to say it.

43

לשׁוֹן

LAMED, SHIN, NUN

TRIPPINGLY ON THE TONGUE

You needn't be a trained linguist — a בַּלְשָׁן (*balshan*) — to count yourself among חוֹבְבֵי שְׂפַת עֵבֶר (*hovevei sefat ever*), "lovers of the Hebrew language." If, however, you do call yourself one or the other, you should be aware of the two different roots of the Hebrew word for "language."

Since languages are spoken before they are set to writing, it should come as no surprise that both words for language are nouns designating the two most important organs of speech, the לָשׁוֹן (*lashon*), "tongue," and the שָׂפָה (*safah*), "lip."

As a verb, the root לשׁן (LAMED, SHIN, NUN) has a form, לְהַלְשִׁין (*le-halshin*), to denote what the Jewish tradition considers a reprehensible activity, "to slander," "to calumniate," "to inform on." So strong is the Jewish aversion to calumny that the daily *Amidah* prayer contains a benediction against it, beginning וְלַמַּלְשִׁינִים אַל תְּהִי תִקְוָה (*ve-la-malshinim al tehi tikvah*), "May slanderers be forlorn." Even slightly more benign acts of speech are frowned upon, as is evident from the idiom for gossip and scandal-mongering, which is called לָשׁוֹן הָרָע (*leshon ha-ra*), literally, "tongue of evil." These negative associations stem from the long-held belief that הַמָּוֶת וְהַחַיִּים בְּיַד הַלָּשׁוֹן (*ha-mavet ve-hahayyim be-yad ha-lashon*), "both death and life are in the grasp of language." What then of life?

A smooth transition from the evil effects of speech to its beneficent use can be found in the Hebrew expression לָשׁוֹן נְקִיָּה (*lashon nekiyah*), "euphemism," literally, "clean language." That the Hebrew language was destined to be used for positive purposes is clear from the way the Rabbis characterized it, לְשׁוֹן־הַקֹּדֶשׁ (*leshon ha-kodesh*), "the tongue of holiness."

Rashi, the eleventh-century French exegete, looking at a Hebrew expression for "Egyptians" in Psalms, עַם לֹעֵז (*am lo-ez*), "a people of strange language," saw in it לע״ז (*la″az*), the abbreviation for לְשׁוֹן עַם זָר (*leshon am zar*), the "language of a foreign nation," that is, French. The modern Hebrew word for "foreign language" is לוֹעֲזִית (*lo'azit*). When the Zionists looked into Psalms, they came back with the famous oath "If I forget thee, O Jerusalem, תִּדְבַּק לְשׁוֹנִי לְחִכִּי [*tidbak leshoni le-hiki*], may my tongue cleave to the roof of my mouth."

One of the most graphic uses of the word לָשׁוֹן (*lashon*) is the Hebrew idiomatic expression לָשׁוֹן נוֹפֵל עַל לָשׁוֹן (*lashon nofel al lashon*), "pun," literally, and at the same time, highly suggestively, "The tongue falls on the tongue."

When the tongue falls on the lips, לָשׁוֹן (*lashon*) becomes שָׂפָה (*safah*). More about the word שָׂפָה (*safah*), "lip," in chapter 96.

44

מאה

MEM, ALEF, HEH

CENTURY NOTES

Numbering, to be sure, is central to all the world's religions, but in none of them, perhaps, is the number 100, מֵאָה (me'ah), more prevalent than in Judaism.

Variations of the word מֵאָה (me'ah) appear in Hebrew Scripture more than five hundred times. Thus, Abraham was בֶּן מְאַת שָׁנָה (ben me'at shanah), "a hundred years old," when Isaac was born. Moses was בֶּן מֵאָה וְעֶשְׂרִים שָׁנָה (ben me'ah ve-esrim shanah), "a hundred and twenty years old," when he died. One hundred and twenty was also the age assigned to mankind in Genesis. Hence the famous Jewish mantra עַד מֵאָה וְעֶשְׂרִים (ad me'ah ve-esrim), "May you live to be a hundred and twenty." A modern witty and playful version of this saying goes like this: עַד מֵאָה כְּמוֹ עֶשְׂרִים (ad me'ah kemo esrim), "May you live to a hundred as though you were twenty."

Wanting to emphasize the biblical notion that two witnesses are necessary and sufficient to establish the truth of a situation, the Rabbis expressed it in the following Aramaic formula: מֵאָה כִּתְרֵי וּתְרֵי כְּמֵאָה (me'ah ke-trei u-trei ke-me'ah), "A hundred witnesses are no better than two and two witnesses are as good as a hundred." The Rabbis were also interested in promoting mass education and, in a slight exaggeration, would point out that it costs no more to educate a hundred students than one. Or as they said it, slightly more poetically,—נֵר לְאֶחָד נֵר לְמֵאָה (ner le-ehad — ner le-me'ah), "A candle that illuminates one person can enlighten a hundred." The rabbinic expression for "a hundred-fold" is the basis for the name of the Jerusalem neighborhood מֵאָה שְׁעָרִים (me'ah she'arim), which originally had one hundred parcels of land.

Organized Jewish life today — as we come to the end of the מֵאָה הָעֶשְׂרִים (me'ah ha-esrim), "the twentieth century" — is run on a very sound capitalistic principle: "The one who pays the piper calls the tune," or, in nicely rhyming Hebrew, בַּעַל הַמֵּאָה הוּא בַּעַל הַדֵּעָה (ba'al ha-

me'ah hu ba'al ha-de'ah), literally, "The owner of the hundred is the owner of the idea."

Using another word for hundred, מָנֶה (*maneh*), the Hebrew language makes a nice psychological point about human nature: יֵשׁ לוֹ מָנֶה רוֹצֶה מָאתַיִם (*yesh lo maneh rotseh matayim*), "If a person has a hundred monetary units, he wants two hundred," or, idiomatically, "The more you have, the more you want." From this author's point of view, that goes for Hebrew words as well.

45
מלל

MEM, LAMED, LAMED
A WORD IS A WORD

One of the more lustily enjoyed activities associated with the Hanukkah season is the unself-conscious singing of Hanukkah songs in the bosom of one's family. The highlight of this evening activity is the intonation with obvious gusto of the round that begins מִי יְמַלֵּל גְּבוּרוֹת יִשְׂרָאֵל (mi yemalel gevurot yisrael), "Who shall recount the heroic deeds of Israel?"

As one can tell from this usage of the infinitive לְמַלֵּל (le-malel), the verb means something more than merely "to tell"; it sometimes takes on the nuance of "to proclaim" or even "to foretell." The verb, taken from Scripture, is rarely used as such in modern Hebrew. It can be found, however, in a "mixed up" form, לְמַלְמֵל (le-malmel), "to babble," where the extra מ (MEM) is intended to reproduce the new word's meaning by both its spelling and its sound.

Nouns formed from the root מלל (MEM, LAMED, LAMED) are more frequent, so much so that they have two forms: מֶלֶל (melel) and מִלָּה (millah), "word." The word מֶלֶל (melel) is found in both the Rosh Hashana liturgy, where it means "praise for the Lord," and the world of modern popular music, where it is sometimes used in the sense of "song lyrics." The dot in the LAMED of the second word, מִלָּה (millah), indicates that one of the original LAMEDs has been cut off. The double "l" in the transliteration indicates that an effort should be made to pronounce the missing letter.

There are those who believe that the word מִלָּה (millah), which is the standard word in Hebrew for the word "word," is related to the ritual act of circumcision, called in Hebrew brit milah. Do these people base themselves on the widely accepted notion that written language originally involved a "cutting" of sorts, usually on stone? Although there is usually some truth in the most wildly outrageous of conjectures, this one seems farfetched in the extreme, בִּמְלֹא מוּבָן הַמִּלָּה (*bimlo muvan ha-millah*), "in the full sense of the word."

In the modern Hebrew spoken on the street, the word מִלָּה (*mil-lah*) also means one's "word of honor," as in the colloquial expression מִלָּה־זֶה־מִלָּה (*millah-zeh-millah*), "You gave your word." You cannot have failed to notice that this last expression was not translated מִלָּה בְּמִלָּה (*millah be-millah*), "word for word," "verbatim." In daily life again, it's always nice to hear a מִלָּה טוֹבָה (*millah tovah*), an "encouraging word." Don't be surprised, however, if every once in a while you hear a number of מִלִּים גַּסּוֹת (*millim gassot*), "vulgar words."

Where, besides the streets of Israel, do you find all these מִלִּים (*millim*), "words"? Why, in a מִלּוֹן (*millon*), a "dictionary," of course, compiled by your local מִלּוֹנַאי (*millona'i*), "lexicographer." You'll also find them in books about Hebrew and, at home, in the mouths of your favorite Hanukkah singers.

46

מנה

MEM, NUN, HEH

A GOODLY PORTION

Did you ever notice how those little foreign-language phrase books for travelers always seem designed for an ideal world, where everybody is polite and scrupulously honest? For example, what do the phrase books tell you to say to a cabdriver in Israel who charmingly neglects to activate the meter, often concealed in the glove compartment? The answer these books don't give is: שִׂים אֶת הַמּוֹנֶה (sim et ha-moneh), "Turn on the meter." After all, you are in a מוֹנִית (monit), "taxicab."

The root מנה (MEM, NUN, HEH) can be traced back to the biblical promise that the People of Israel will be so numerous that only a person who is able לִמְנוֹת (limnot), "to count," the dust of the earth will be able to count the Jews. The Hanukkah song alluded to in the previous chapter asks not only "Who can recount?" but also מִי יִמְנֶה (mi yimneh), "Who can count?" A completely different biblical use of the root is found in the Book of Jonah, where the phrase וַיְמַן (va-yeman), "[the Lord] appointed," is used to single out the "big fish," the gourd, the worm, and the wind chosen to fulfill God's purpose.

Both senses of the word are found in everyday Hebrew today. We all know that a מִנְיָן (minyan) is a "quorum" of ten Jews required for communal prayer. At the Hebrew University in Jerusalem, a פְּרוֹפֶסוֹר מִן הַמִּנְיָן (profesor min ha-minyan) is not an academic who attends prayer services at the Hecht Synagogue on campus but rather one who has been appointed a "full professor."

As we learned in a previous chapter, there was a time when the root signified not ten but one hundred. This is obvious from the rabbinic dictum about human cupidity, a dictum that bears repeating: יֵשׁ לוֹ מָנֶה רוֹצֶה מָאתַיִם (yesh lo maneh, rotseh matayim), "A person who has a מָנֶה (maneh), one hundred, always wants two hundred."

Do not, however, confuse מָנֶה (maneh) with מָנָה (manah), "portion."

This word is used in the plural on Purim to designate the *mitsvah* of מִשְׁלוֹחַ מָנוֹת (*mishloah manot*), the "sending of edible gifts," and in the singular in Israeli restaurants to designate the courses of a meal, such as the מָנָה רִאשׁוֹנָה (*manah rishonah*), "entree," מָנָה עִיקָרִית (*manah ikarit*), "main course," and מָנָה אַחֲרוֹנָה (*manah aharonah*), "dessert." It is also found in the prepositional phrase עַל מְנָת (*al menat*), "in order to," as in the following ethical injunction: Do not perform an act of loving-kindness, עַל מְנָת לְקַבֵּל פְּרַס (*al menat le-kabel peras*), "in order to receive a reward."

If you go to Israel for an extended stay, it is recommended that you reward yourself with a מִנּוּי (*minui*) or two, either a "subscription" to the theater or a "membership" in a swimming pool. You also might want to consider purchasing a few מְנָיוֹת (*menayot*) – plural of מְנָיָה (*menayah*) – "shares" in an Israeli company. Of course, that's recommended only for people who have already mastered Israeli מוֹנִיּוֹת (*moniot*), "taxicabs."

47

נגד

NUN, GIMMEL, DALET

AGAINST AGAINST

Everybody knows that the name of the book used for conducting the Passover Seder is the הַגָּדָה (*haggadah*). Some can even cite the source in Scripture from which the word *haggadah* is derived. Rare is the person, however, who knows the enigmatic root of this oh-so-common word.

The source of the noun הַגָּדָה (*haggadah*) is the verse in Exodus that enjoins parents to relate to their children the miracles that God wrought for their ancestors in Egypt: וְהִגַּדְתָּ לְבִנְךָ (*ve-higgadeta le-vinkha*), "You shall tell your son." Thus it is that one of the main *mitsvot* of Passover is the telling of stories. In fact, one of the most important sections of the Seder is called מַגִּיד (*maggid*), "telling." In Eastern Europe, a *maggid* was an itinerant preacher and storyteller. The word הַגָּדָה (*haggadah*) has an Aramaic cousin, אַגָּדָה (*aggadah*), "narrative."

The root of the verb לְהַגִּיד (*le-haggid*), "to tell," is not at all easy to guess. The double "g" in the transliteration hints that a letter has dropped by the wayside. That letter is a נ (NUN), leading us to speculate that the original infinitive was the unattested form לְהַנְגִיד (*le-hangid*). The existence of the noun הַנְגָּדָה (*hangadah*), "confrontation," not only lends credence to the hypothesis but also gets us closer to the root נגד (NUN, GIMMEL, DALET), as in the preposition נֶגֶד (*neged*), "against." How did it come about that "to tell" and "to oppose" were derived from the same root?

The verb נָגַד (*nagad*) originally meant "to be conspicuous," "to be apparent"—as we would say today, "to be up front." Just as someone who is נֶגֶד (*neged*), "directly opposite," another is conspicuous to him, so too someone who takes pains לְהַגִּיד (*le-haggid*), "to relate," an event places it "up front" in the listener's consciousness.

In the biblical description of Eve as an עֵזֶר כְּנֶגְדוֹ (*ezer ke-negdo*), a help "meet" for Adam, our word means not opposite but appropriate.

When Moses is told that he will not enter the Promised Land but will merely see it, the Torah specifies that he will do so מִנֶּגֶד (mi-negged), "from afar." In Jewish history, when you speak of הַנָּגִיד (ha-nagid), the "prince" or "leader," you are referring to the great medieval rabbi Shmuel the Prince. In Israel today you would be talking about the governor of the Bank of Israel. To return to the Haggadah, in its presentation of the *aggadah* of the four sons, we are told that the Torah speaks כְּנֶגֶד (ke-neged), "in relation to," four sons.

It is curious how often Jewish culture and values seem to be on a wavelength different from the rest of the world. According to one Israeli thinker, this stems from the Jewish people's need and willingness to swim נֶגֶד הַזֶּרֶם (neged ha-zerem), "against the flow." Nevertheless, whether you are a descendant of a hasidic *maggid* or of the מִתְנַגְדִים (mitnagdim), "opponents" of the *hasidim*, your use of Hebrew will attenuate the difference.

48

נוח

NUN, VAV, HET

REST AND RECREATION

When a Jewish parent says, "All I want from my children is a little *naches*," other parents sense — without even knowing the Hebrew derivation of the word *naches* — what is meant by the Yiddish term. Indeed, you don't have to know that in Hebrew נַחַת (*nahat*) derives from the root נוח (NUN, VAV, HET), "to rest," to want to derive pleasure from your children.

How does one get from "rest" to "satisfaction"? In the Torah, it is only when we get to the Book of Exodus, in the Ten Commandments, that we learn that God rested, וַיִּנָּח (*va-yanah*), on the seventh day. In Genesis the verbs used are וַיְכַל (*va-yekhal*) and וַיִּשְׁבֹּת (*va-yishbot*), "He stopped" and "He abstained." The first recorded instance of resting using our root is applied to Noah's ark, in the phrase וַתָּנַח הַתֵּבָה (*va-tanah ha-tevah*), "The ark came to rest" (on Mount Ararat).

The root is also found in Psalm 23, used in both Judaism and Christianity in the consolation mode. One of the best known of the biblical liturgies read mainly at funerals, the Psalm helps us to express confidence that God will lead us beside מֵי מְנֻחוֹת (*mei menuhot*), "still waters."

In Hebrew grammar and phonetics, a "mute e," that is, a vowel that is not pronounced, is called a שְׁוָא נָח (*sheva nah*), or, as the linguists say, a "quiescent *schwa*." In scientific Hebrew, the technical term for a "technical term" is a מוּנָח (*munah*), that is, a word "laid down" for you by an authority with expertise.

To "lay down," a transitive verb, is one of the major uses of the root, especially in the verb לְהָנִיחַ (*le-haniah*). A הֲנָחָה (*hanahah*) is a "reduction" in price (designed to give you relief from inflated prices); a הַנָּחָה (*hannahah*), note the dot in the NUN, is an "assumption" you make when laying down a hypothesis. To complicate matters further, don't confuse הַנָּחָה (*hannahah*), "assumption," with הַנְחָיָה (*hanhayah*), "directive." This last you receive from a מַנְחֶה (manheh), "leader" of a group or "chairman" of a meeting.

Speaking of meetings, the next time one of yours gets a bit tense or tedious, why not ask the מַנְחֶה (manheh) for an אֶתְנַחְתָּא (etnahta)? This is an Aramaic term, found most commonly today in Bible-cantillation manuals, designating a brief pause in the recitation of a verse, something like a comma in a sentence. In modern Hebrew, it is used to designate a "break" in the proceedings. If the meeting is long enough, sometimes you need an אֶתְנַחְתָּא (etnahta) to let people go to the נוֹחִיּוּת (nohiut), the "comfort station," a beautiful Hebrew euphemism for bathroom. In the Torah section dealing with sacrifices, a burnt sacrifice is said to give off a רֵיחַ נִיחוֹחַ (reiah nihoah), an "agreeable odor." It is debatable how many modern Jews would agree to that proposition.

Although *naches* from children provides pleasure of a completely different order, it should be clearer now how resting can lead to comfort and take us from there to satisfaction and pleasure.

49
נטל

NUN, TET, LAMED

TAKE THE *LULAV*...PLEASE

What do shaking the *lulav* on Sukkot and pouring water over your hands before the holiday or *Shabbat* meal (or, for that matter, before any meal) have in common? A good question. After all, both acts are accompanied by a blessing containing the same word, נְטִילָה (*netilah*): עַל נְטִילַת לוּלָב (*al netilat lulav*), and עַל נְטִילַת יָדַיִם (*al netilat yadayim*). Given this commonality, shall we not conclude that the essence of these ritual acts is neither "shaking" nor "pouring" but נְטִילָה (*netilah*), whatever that is.

And what is נְטִילָה (*netilah*)? A sense of "taking" can be deduced from the two verbs used by the prophet Isaiah to describe God's historic protection of the people of Israel, וַיְנַטְלֵם וַיְנַשְּׂאֵם (*va-yinatlem va-yinas'em*), "He bore them and He carried them."

A further clue is available from the biblical injunction that on Sukkot וּלְקַחְתֶּם לָכֶם (*u-lekahtem lakhem*), "You shall take to yourselves" the four species that make up the *lulav* and *etrog*. The roots לָקַח (*lakah*) in the Torah and נָטַל (*natal*) in the *berakhah* would both mean "to take." And washing the hands? A clue here is available from the Aramaic word נַטְלָא (*natla*), "ladle," used to transfer water from a larger vessel. This is similar to the Hebrew word for the beautiful ceramic or metal נַטְלָה (*natlah*), "laver," used in pouring the water over the hands. A more direct explanation is that נְטִילַת יָדַיִם (*netilat yadayim*) is a "taking of the hands" from the realm of the impure into the realm of the pure, readying them for the ritual blessing of the bread.

Something that is borne is often weighty, and this is the sense of the noun נֵטֶל (*neitel*), "heaviness," and the adjective נָטִיל (*natil*), "loaded." Interestingly, the way the prophet Zephaniah describes those who are, as the Yiddish slang has it, *ungeshtupt mit gelt*, "loaded with money," is נְטִילֵי כֶּסֶף (*netilei khessef*), "wealthy."

Taking can also mean taking away. The sense of removal can be found in modern Hebrew in, of all places, your kitchen pantry, specifi-cally in your "decaffeinated" coffee, which is נָטוּל קָפֵאִין (*natul kafei'in*).

In Hebrew grammar, at least, what you take you can also put. An active form of the verb is לְהַטִיל (*le-hatil*), "to cast." This form can be found in expressions as widely divergent as לְהַטִיל מִסִּים (*le-hatil missim*), "to impose taxes," and לְהַטִיל בֵּיצָה (*le-hatil beitsah*), "to lay an egg."

Whether an egg or taxes, one's hands or a *lulav*, all would agree that it's also good, once in a while, to take.

50
נשא

NUN, SIN, ALEF

PRESIDENTS AND PURIM

A distinguishing mark of Israel's form of government is that not only does it have a רֹאשׁ מֶמְשָׁלָה (*rosh memshalah*), a "head of government" but it has as well a נָשִׂיא (*nasi*), "president," who serves as the head of state.

The term נָשִׂיא (*nasi*) is firmly rooted in the beginnings of the Jewish people, when the chiefs of the biblical tribes of Israel were called נְשִׂיאִים (*nesi'im*). Later generations were to use the word — ever so flexible — to designate the head of the Sanhedrin, the most famous of whom was רַבִּי יְהוּדָה הַנָּשִׂיא (*rabbi yehudah ha-nasi*), Rabbi Judah the Prince.

The root נשא (NUN, SIN, ALEF) means "to carry," "to raise," "to take," "to forgive," and "to be married," among other meanings. Verbal richness, however, can lead to ambiguity — and requires much attention to context. Depending on where it is used, the expression meaning literally to raise someone's head, נָשָׂא אֶת רֹאשׁוֹ (*nasa et rosho*), can mean: "He was promoted," "He was decapitated," "He was pardoned," or "He was counted."

Isaiah's beautiful prophecy that "nation shall not lift sword against nation" is expressed in Hebrew with our verb לֹא יִשָּׂא גוֹי אֶל גוֹי חֶרֶב (*lo yisa goi el goi herev*). And, speaking of prophecy, one of the ten biblical terms for that activity is מַשָּׂא (*masa*), yet another derivation. The Rabbis explain that this term, whose original sense is "burden," is reserved for prophecies that have heavy consequences.

The prohibition against swearing falsely comes from both our root and the Third Commandment, לֹא תִשָּׂא אֶת שֵׁם ה'...לַשָּׁוְא (*lo tisa et shem ha-shem . . . la-shav*), "You shall not take God's name in vain." Our root also reminds us that, because God is forgiving, some prophecies are fallible. In the liturgy of the High Holy Days, we repeat frequently the verse נוֹשֵׂא עָוֹן וָפֶשַׁע (*noseh avon va-fesha*), God "forgives sins and misdeeds," that is, "He bears them away."

We often like to think, romantically perhaps, that marriage is a kind of "carrying away," and the word for marriage, נִשּׂוּאִים (nisuim), adds substance to that thought. In modern Israeli slang a devoted husband is sometimes called, jokingly, נָשׂוּי לְגַמְרֵי (nasui le-gamrei), "thoroughly married." And in America we constantly hear of נִשּׂוּאֵי תַּעֲרֹבֶת (nisuei ta'arovet), "mixed marriages."

Depending on the context, both the head of state and the head of government in Israel find it congenial to engage in מַשָּׂא וּמַתָּן (massa u-matan), "negotiations," an activity that always seems to be going on in the Middle East. Or if we are more interested in Purim, we can always boo the verse in the Book of Esther 3:1, when, using the verb וַיְנַשְּׂאֵהוּ (va-yenaseihu), Ahasuerus "raises" Haman figuratively above his other ministers. In either case, the Hebrew language is never far from Jewish politics.

51

נֶפֶשׁ

NUN, FEH, SHIN

THE SOUL OF THE MATTER

There is a custom during the weeks preceding the Day of Judgment (Yom Kippur) to engage in personal soul-searching. This understandably neglected custom is called in Hebrew חֶשְׁבּוֹן הַנֶּפֶשׁ (*heshbon ha-nefesh*), "reckoning of the soul." If, for reasons known only to ourselves, we dare not examine our conscience for fear of what we might find, we can nevertheless have a look at the wide spectrum of meanings and expressive images connected with the word נֶפֶשׁ (*nefesh*), "soul."

First of all, it doesn't mean only soul. Depending on the context, the word נֶפֶשׁ (*nefesh*) can allude to anything that breathes, to a character in the cast of a play, or even to a monument for the dead.

On the fifth day of Creation, as recounted in the Book of Genesis, the first living creatures are called נֶפֶשׁ חַיָּה (*nefesh hayyah*). The explanation for one of the strictest taboos in the Torah – against the eating of blood – states that הַדָּם הוּא הַנֶּפֶשׁ (*ha-dam hu ha-nefesh*), "blood is the soul." While most civilized people would balk at exacting "an eye for an eye" in civil cases, there are those who are in favor of the death penalty in דִּינֵי נְפָשׁוֹת (*dinei nefashot*), "capital offenses." Curiously, the biblical expression נֶפֶשׁ תַּחַת נֶפֶשׁ (*nefesh tahat nafesh*) does not mean, according to the Rabbis, "a life for a life" but rather refers to monetary payment. The Jewish value system does not like to exact the death penalty, even if it does like to keep it on the books.

That the נֶפֶשׁ (*nefesh*) is at the root of human emotions can be seen in the modern Hebrew expression heard in exceptionally polite company, עֲשֵׂה כְּנַפְשֶׁךָ (*aseh ke-nafshekha*), "Act according to your heart's desire," or, somewhat more idiomatically, "Consider yourself at home." If you're squeamish at the sight of disorder, you would probably find the room of a teenage boy גֹּעַל נֶפֶשׁ (*go-al nefesh*), "disgusting." The idiom חוֹלֶה נֶפֶשׁ (*holeh nefesh*), "mental patient," is an expression in which נֶפֶשׁ (*nefesh*) means "mind." Aharon Appelfed's first novel published in English, *Badenheim 1939*, hauntingly describes Jewish insouciance at an עִיר נֹפֶשׁ (*ir nofesh*), "resort town," on the eve of the Holocaust.

Sometimes words and expressions change meanings with the times. Until recently, the expression יְפֵה נֶפֶשׁ (*yefeh nefesh*), literally "a beauty of a soul," was used to describe a person of refined sensibilities. Nowadays it is used scornfully to denigrate a "bleeding-heart liberal." On the other hand, a person heavily engaged in volunteer work is characterized by his or her מְסִירוּת נֶפֶשׁ (*mesirut nefesh*), the "giving over of the soul" to good causes.

When God finished creating the world, we are told that on the seventh day שָׁבַת וַיִּנָּפַשׁ (*shavat va-yinafash*), "He ceased work and withdrew into Himself." Interestingly, according to tradition, on *Shabbat* we are given both a supplementary soul and second word for soul, a נְשָׁמָה יְתֵרָה (*neshamah yeteirah*), in which the word נְשָׁמָה (*neshamah*) plays the same role as נֶפֶשׁ (*nefesh*).

What this means, perhaps, is that we have little to fear from a חֶשְׁבּוֹן הַנֶּפֶשׁ (*heshbon ha-nefesh*), a "reckoning of the soul." Should we find our first נֶפֶשׁ (*nefesh*) wanting, we always have our second נְשָׁמָה (*neshamah*) to fall back on.

52

נצח

NUN, TSADI, HET

FROM NOW TO ETERNITY

When does a slogan become a trend? In response to the success of שָׁלוֹם עַכְשָׁו (*shalom akhshav*), "Peace Now," as both a slogan and a movement, there has recently appeared a new graffito on the walls in Israel: שָׁלוֹם לָנֶצַח (*shalom la-netzah*), "everlasting peace."

The root נצח (NUN, TSADI, HET), when used as a verb, has several senses, among them, "to last forever," "to conquer," "to lead in music," and "to glorify."

There is an edifying story in the Talmud, used as a proof text by those who wish to show that Judaism is anthropocentric, in which our root plays a prominent role. It gives the impression that there are times in God's relationship with man when He is pleased to be vanquished. When the Rabbis "prove" from a biblical verse that their majority decision takes precedence over even the divine voice from Heaven, God is quoted as saying, with obvious glee, נִצְחוּנִי בָּנַי (*nitshuni banai*), "My children have defeated me."

The sense of leadership is found in a noun common to the modern concert hall and Scripture. A מְנַצֵּחַ (*menatse'ah*) is not only a "victor" but also a sort of "musical director." The first word of 54 of the 150 psalms is לַמְנַצֵּחַ (*la-menatse'ah*), "To the conductor."

When a Jewish text wishes to insist that some activity is to be long-lasting, one of the linguistic tactics it uses is to double our root: לְנֶצַח נְצָחִים (*le-netsah netsahim*), "for ever and ever." The word נֶצַח (*netsah*) holds an honored place in Zionist history. The acronym "Nili" – from the prophetic verse, נֵצַח יִשְׂרָאֵל לֹא יְשַׁקֵּר (*netsah yisrael lo yishaker*), "The eternal [God] of Israel will not abrogate His word" – was the password for and the name of Aaron and Sarah Aaronsohn's pro-British spying organization during World War I.

The root can also be found in a Hebrew formulation of the Christian concept of the Wandering Jew, הַיְּהוּדִי הַנִּצְחִי (*ha-yehudi ha-*

nits'hi), literally, the "eternal Jew." The Jewish confrontation with change is problematic because many Jews maintain that there are such things as עֲרָכִים נִצְחִיִּים (*arakhim nits'hiim*), "eternal values," derived from a סֵפֶר נִצְחִי (*sefer nitshi*), an "everlasting book." Virtually all Jews look to Jerusalem as their בִּירַת נֶצַח (*birat netsah*), "eternal capital."

To get back to the sense of victory and its glorification, all nations use monuments, such as a שַׁעַר נִצָּחוֹן (*sha'ar nitsahon*), a "triumphal arch," to commemorate victories in battle. Since the word for arch is also the Hebrew for both "gate" and "goal," Israeli sports fans, much given to colorful slang, use the expression שַׁעַר נִצָּחוֹן (*sha'ar nitsahon*) to denote the tiebreaking goal in a soccer match.

In war especially, it is important to avoid a נִצָּחוֹן פִּירוּס (*nits'hon pirus*), a "Pyrrhic victory," which brings neither "peace now" nor "everlasting peace."

53

סדר

SAMEKH, DALET, RESH

EVERYTHING IN ORDER

How is the festive meal of Passover different from the meal eaten at other holiday celebrations? For one thing, the Passover repast is consumed in the context of a scripted dramatic arrangement, a סֵדֶר (seder), from the Hebrew verb לְסַדֵּר (le-sadder), "to arrange."

There are, to be sure, similar arrangements in Jewish ritual and textual life. The daily prayer book, which contains a sort of script for the performance of devotional texts, is called a סִדּוּר (siddur). One of the names of the weekly Torah portion read in synagogue is the סִדְרָה (sidra), from the Aramaic cognate of the root. The Mishna is divided into six סְדָרִים (sedarim), "orders"; the one containing the laws of Passover is called סֵדֶר מוֹעֵד (seder mo'ed), the "Order of the Festivals."

The root סדר (SAMEKH, DALET, RESH) is found in many more or less organized situations. If you volunteer to work on a kibbutz in Israel, the most important person to know is not the kibbutz מַזְכִּיר (mazkir), "secretary," but the סַדְרָן הָעֲבוֹדָה (sadran ha-avodah), the "foreman" who distributes the daily assignments. The word סַדְרָן (sadran) is also used in Israeli theaters for an "usher," but, to be perfectly candid, what most of us have experienced in these settings is אִי־סֵדֶר (i seder), "disorder."

An אָדָם מְסֻדָּר (adam mesudar) is an "orderly person," and, by extension into colloquial Hebrew, someone who is well off financially. Of a person who always lands on his feet, one says הוּא יוֹדֵעַ לְהִסְתַּדֵּר (hu yode'a le-histadder). One of the most important institutions in Israeli social and communal life is the הִסְתַּדְּרוּת (histadrut), the "Federation of Labor." In America, an important organization — with a glorious history — for the promotion of the Hebrew language is the הִסְתַּדְּרוּת עִבְרִית (histadrut ivrit), whose meetings are always governed by a סֵדֶר־הַיּוֹם (seder ha-yom), an "agenda."

The expressiveness of a Hebrew root can often be found in its colloquial use. In the matter of human rights, for example, the Soviets were said to be לֹא בְּסֵדֶר (*lo be-seder*), an excessively polite way of accusing them of gross impropriety. When one reads Natan Sharansky's historic closing words at his 1978 trial, one wants to burst with pride that הוּא סִדֵּר אוֹתָם (*hu sidder otam*), "he really gave it to them." It is perhaps no coincidence that the first Hebrew words spoken by Sharansky on his arrival in Israel were הַכֹּל בְּסֵדֶר (*ha-kol be-seder*), "Everything's all right."

At your next Passover *Seder*, as you meditate on the heroism demonstrated by Sharansky in his exodus from slavery to freedom, and on his being able to celebrate "next year in Jerusalem," you will be able to believe – if only for a moment – that something is indeed בְּסֵדֶר (*be-seder*) with this world.

54

סִים

SAMEKH, YOD, MEM

IN CONCLUSION

Did you ever notice how people rush to celebrate conclusions, even of something whose duration they enjoy? In the month of June, for example (if not already in May), students the world over celebrate the conclusion of their studies. In Israel, in this respect a country like any other, a graduation celebration is called a חַג הַסִּיּוּם (*hag ha-siyum*). In the traditional Jewish world, a world apart, to be sure, the conclusion of the study of a tractate of the Talmud is also celebrated by a סִיּוּם (*siyum*), in which whiskey and sponge cake replace the cap and gown.

There seems to be a difference of opinion as to the exact root of our word. Is it סוּם (SAMEKH, VAV, MEM) or סִים (SAMEKH, YOD, MEM)? In rabbinic Hebrew, the former root meant "to attach," or "to tie together." A סוּמָא (*suma*), a "blind person," was one whose eyes had been, figuratively, tied closed. In modern Hebrew, the latter root means "to end," "to finish," "to terminate," as in the above-mentioned סִיּוּם (*siyyum*). Apparently, both of these roots contain within them the meaning of "to mark," "to designate," and may be related to yet another word, סִימָן (*siman*), a "sign" or a "symbol."

This meaning is best illustrated in the adjective derived from our root, מְסֻיָּם (*mesuyyam*), "certain," "definite." In the Talmud we learn that בְּהֵמָה יוֹלֶדֶת לְחֳדָשִׁים מְסֻיָּמִים (*behemah yoledet la-hodashim mesuyyamim*), "an animal gives birth after a certain number of completed months," where מְסֻיָּם (*mesuyyam*) means both "certain" and "completed." In modern Hebrew the adjective is found, to a certain degree, in expressions like בְּמִדָּה מְסֻיֶּמֶת (*be-middah mesuyyemet*), "to a certain degree."

In Hebrew grammar a סִיֹּמֶת (*siyyomet*), "suffix," is distinguished from a קִדֹּמֶת (*kidomet*), "prefix," this last word also being used for a telephone area code.

Another way of marking off the meaning of our word is to look

---

at its verb form, most frequently in the pi'el, סִיֵּם (*siyyem*), "He ended." Interestingly the verb is often found in expressions that contain the opposite verb, פָּתַח (*patah*), "He opened." Thus, when we want to talk of someone whose speech (and writing?) wanders all over the place, we say פָּתַח בְּכַד וְסִיֵּם בְּחָבִית (*patah be-khad ve-siyyem be-havit*), literally, "He opened with a 'pitcher' and ended with a 'barrel.'"

To all מְסַיְּמִים (*mesaymim*), "graduates," may the future provide both pitchers and barrels of good things, and the wisdom to understand that we celebrate endings because they are also beginnings.

55

סְעַד

SAMEKH, AYIN, DALET

FOOD AND WELFARE

Some roots – firmly implanted in the language as nouns – have a difficult time grafting themselves on to daily speech as verbs. Take the example of the verb לִסְעֹד (lis'od), "to dine," from the root סעד (SAMEKH, AYIN, DALET), "to support," "to assist."

In the old days, according to Israeli children's poet Yehuda Atlas, the verb לִסְעֹד (lis'od) could indeed be found on the lips of children, but only in didactic children's literature, not in real life. At that time and in those stories, when a child wanted to ask his mother for breakfast, he would say, according to Atlas, אִמִּי אֲנִי חָפֵץ לִסְעֹד פַּת שַׁחֲרִית (immi ani hafets lis'od pat shaharit). An English equivalent of that sentence might be, "Mother mine, I desire to dine on the morning loaf." Of course, no child ever spoke like that.

In Israel today, the root סעד (SAMEKH, AYIN DALET) is encountered either in the lovely קִבּוּץ סַעַד (kibbuts sa'ad), not far from Gaza, in the מַחְלֶקֶת הַסְּעוּד (mahleket ha-siyud), "nursing department" of a hospital, or when someone needs the help of the מִשְׂרַד הַסַּעַד (misrad ha-sa'ad), the "Ministry of Social Welfare." All Israelis, rich or poor, know what a מִסְעָדָה (mis'adah), "restaurant," is, either because they eat out frequently or because they have seen one of the funniest and most socially relevant programs on Israeli television. Called הַמִּסְעָדָה הַגְּדוֹלָה (ha-mis'adah ha-gedolah), "The Big Restaurant," it showed a friendly restaurant where Hebrew and Arabic were spoken interchangeably.

The meal you eat in a restaurant is called a סְעֻדָּה (se'udah), but that's not the only place you eat it. In many synagogues, late on a Saturday afternoon, a light meal, called shaleshudes in American Yiddish, is served. In reality, this is the סְעֻדָּה הַשְּׁלִישִׁית (se'udah ha-shelishit), the "third meal" of the three we are commanded to eat on Shabbat.

There are many religiously ordained meals in Judaism. Many families gather for a סְעֻדַּת פּוּרִים (se'udat purim), "Purim meal," just as we gather for any סְעֻדַּת מִצְוָה (se'udat mitsvah), "ceremonial meal," on joyous occasions such as at a wedding, a circumcision, or the completion of a study cycle. The meal taken before a fast, as on Erev Yom Kippur, is called the סְעֻדָה הַמַּפְסֶקֶת (se'udah ha-mafseket), the "stopping meal."

The root is found in proper names as well, from tenth-century Jewish sage and scholar סַעַדְיָה גָאוֹן (sa'adyah ga'on), where the term means "God is my support," to non-Jews such as twelfth-century Persian nature poet Sa'adi and contemporary Columbia University English professor Edward Said, formerly a member of the Palestine National Council. Is it possible that this last name will be made into a verb that will promote the welfare of two nations? Only time will tell.

56

סֵפֶר

SAMEKH, FEH, RESH

COUNTING AND RECOUNTING

There are two types of Jews in this world: the mathematical and the literary, those who crunch numbers and those who tell stories. Telling and tallying, counting and recounting, are pairs of cognates in English. The language of the Jews has a similar pair as well. The verbs לִסְפֹּר (*lispor*), "to count," and לְסַפֵּר (*le-saper*), "to tell," both stem from the root ספר (SAMEKH, FEH, RESH).

Counting has a venerable tradition as a Jewish activity. When Abram, childless, points out to God that it would be difficult for him to be father of his people if he were to remain childless, he is told to count the stars for an idea of the extent of his progeniture. The period between Passover and Shavuot is called סְפִירָה (*sefirah*), during which we count the forty-nine days between the Exodus and the giving of the Ten Commandments.

The word סֵפֶר (*sefer*) means "book" nowadays. Before Gutenberg, it was also a "letter" or "epistle" (as in Esther 9:30) or simply a "document," as in סֵפֶר כְּרִיתוּת (*sefer keritut*), a "bill of divorcement." The focus of Jerusalem's Shrine of the Book is not on books at all but on scrolls. More than one סֵפֶר לָבָן (*sefer lavan*), "White Paper," played an important role in the history of Mandatory Palestine. And, of course, the סֵפֶר הַזָּהָב (*sefer ha-zahav*) is the Jewish National Fund's "Golden Book."

The Jews were called עַם הַסֵּפֶר (*am ha-sefer*), "the people of the book," by Muhammed. A Jewish school is called a בֵּית הַסֵּפֶר (*beit ha-sefer*), literally, a "house of the book." That place where books are kept, ready for use by the public, is called a סִפְרִיָּה (*sifriyyah*), "library," and that wonderful person who takes care of books and makes sure they get into the right hands is a סַפְרָן (*safran*) or a סַפְרָנִית (*safranit*), "librarian." A learned person is called a יוֹדֵעַ סֵפֶר (*yode'a sefer*) or a יוֹדַעַת סֵפֶר (*yoda'at sefer*), a "knower of the book." Israeli newspapers and magazines have a section for בִּקֹּרֶת סְפָרִים (*bikoret sefarim*), "book reviews," where you will find many good titles of modern Jewish סִפֹּרֶת (*sipporet*), "fiction," or of סִפְרוּת (*sifrut*), "literature," written by our best סוֹפְרִים (*sofrim*), "authors."

The root has what appears to be a third cognate, סַפָּר (*sappar*), "barber." Here again, there are two types of Jews: those who believe that סַפָּר (*sappar*) is related to "telling" and "counting" and those who believe that it should be in a different chapter altogether.

What do we think? More about סַפָּר (*sappar*) in the next chapter.

57

ספר

SAMEKH, FEH, RESH

CUTTING THE EDGE

What connection – if any – is there among לִסְפֹּר (lispor), "to count," לְסַפֵּר (le-sapper), "to tell," and לְסַפֵּר (le-sapper), "to cut hair?"

Popular etymologies, especially with a tinge of wry humor, abound. If you walk into מִסְתַּפְּרִים אֵצֶל בָּרוּךְ (mistaprim etsel barukh), "Get Your Haircuts at Barukh's Place," in Ra'anana, the סַפָּר (sappar), "barber," in his מִסְפָּרָה (misparah), "barbershop," will regale you with endless סִפּוּרִים (sippurim), "stories." When he gives you a תִּסְפֹּרֶת (tisporet), "haircut," with his מִסְפָּרַיִם (misparayim), "scissors," does he not always seem to be counting the number of customers waiting for their "next"?

As farfetched and as trivializing as they may seem, these folk etymologies may yet contain a grain of truth. In Hebrew etymology, it is difficult not to take into account that the roots are identical.

It is also important to recognize that originally, writing itself – on clay or wax – involved cutting or carving with a stylus. To "style" a story and to "style" hair may well be related activities. And סַפָּרוּת (saparut) is not only "barbering" but also the "dressing" or "styling" of hair.

There are, of course, other opinions. Some hold that although seemingly related, the words in question are of completely different origins and are therefore to be listed separately. One possibility is that the word לְסַפֵּר (le-sapper), "to cut," is a cognate of the Aramaic סְפַר (se-far), "border," that is, a line that marks the limits between two countries. In this sense, לְהִסְתַּפֵּר (le-histapper), "to get one's hair cut," is in reality to have the edges of one's hair defined, delimited.

Alternatively, there is the possibility that לְסַפֵּר (le-sapper) comes from לְשַׁפֵּר (le-shapper), "to improve," "to adorn," "to beautify." This root may seem a bit "touched up" just for our purposes. Sometimes, however, one must go far to come back to one's roots.

And speaking of borders and improvements, a cartoon that appeared in the Israeli newspaper *Ha-aretz* in the summer of 1994 created the perfect link between modern Middle East geopolitics and the Jewish textual tradition. On the first page of the newspaper was a color photo of Prime Minister Yitzhak Rabin and Jordan's King Hussein cutting a ribbon at the entrance to Aqaba. On the third page was a cartoon whose legend, playing on Micah's beautiful prophecy of peace that proclaims that nations will no longer learn warfare, read: וְכִתְּתוּ חַרְבֹתֵיהֶם...לְמִסְפָּרַיִם (*ve-khitetu harvoteihem le-* . . . *misparayim*), "And they shall beat their swords into . . . scissors."

Readers and writers of books about Hebrew words are always in the presence of אִמְרֵי שֶׁפֶר (*imrei shefer*), "sayings of beauty." Who could ask for anything more?

58

עדן

AYIN, DALET, NUN

THE GARDEN OF PLEASURE

There is a popular belief that when a civilization (or a nation or an ethnic group) attaches extraordinary importance to a particular behavior, it creates a whole spectrum of synonyms for that behavior.

If one were to judge by the number of Hebrew synonyms for the notion of "pleasure" – there are at least a dozen, from תַּעֲנוּג (ta'anug) to הֲנָאָה (hana'ah) to the slangy כֵּיף (keif) – one might think that Judaism was a branch of hedonism.

One of the more fascinating of those synonyms is עֶדְנָה (ednah), a word that appears for the first and only time in Scripture in the story about the way our matriarch Sarah reacted to the news that she would become a mother. There, in Genesis 18:12, when she is told that she is to bear a child, Sarah exclaims: "Is it to be that at my advanced age הָיְתָה לִי עֶדְנָה (haytah li ednah), I shall have pleasure?" The commentators are hard-pressed to explain why Sarah would have chosen the word עֶדְנָה (ednah) here. Was she describing ovulation and menses, a physiological and clinical condition, or was she describing happiness, a psychological state? Whatever the explanation, careful readers of English will recognize the name Edna as deriving from our root.

The root, עדן (AYIN, DALET, NUN), appears in a different context several chapters earlier in Genesis. In chapter 2 we are told that after God had created Adam and Eve, He planted a garden in a place "east of Eden" for man and woman to dwell. This Garden of Eden is known in Hebrew as גַּן עֵדֶן (gan eden), a "pleasure garden," as we can now understand it. In the Talmud, גַּן עֵדֶן (gan eden) is the name of the promised world-to-come. Today's Israelis, when they wax rhapsodic about the place where they live, speak of it as גַּן עֵדֶן עֲלֵי אֲדָמוֹת (gan eden alei adamaot), "paradise on earth." The brand name of Israeli mineral water is מֵי עֵדֶן (mei eden), the "Waters of Eden."

An adjective derived from our root, עָדִין (adin) and עֲדִינָה (adinah,

---

feminine), means "delicate," "refined." The name Adina has been wide-spread in Jewish circles for at least a generation. The masculine name Adin is now becoming popular thanks to the growing prestige of Tal-mud scholar Adin Steinsaltz, one of whose more obvious qualities is his עֲדִינוּת (*adinut*), "refinement."

If you want some good pastry in Israel, don't hesitate to walk into your neighborhood מַעֲדָנִיָּה (*ma'adaniyah*), "delicacy shop." In a Sabbath table hymn written by medieval Hebrew poet Solomon Ibn Gabirol, the Sabbath is described as God's delight, a party to which He invites His creations. According to the words of the song, God says to His people עִדְנוּ מַעֲדָנַי (*idnu ma'adanai*), "Take pleasure in My good things."

Hedonists? Not likely. Pleasure takers? Absolutely.

59

עלה

AYIN, LAMED, HEH

IF NOT HIGHER

The Israeli emissary to the United States was trying, as tactfully as possible, to address a delicate subject: עֲלִיָּה (*aliyah*), "immigration to Israel": "It appears you Americans have *two* types of *aliyah*: going up to Israel to live and going on a visit once or twice a year." Linguistically, at least, the emissary was on target. For if one gives the matter some thought, there are not only two types of *aliyah* but five.

There is first, to be sure, עֲלִיָּה לָאָרֶץ (*aliyah la-arets*), the Hebrew expression for "going up" to the Land of Israel to dwell and settle in it. There is also the shorter עֲלִיָּה לְרֶגֶל (*aliyah le-regel*), the "pilgrimage" up to Jerusalem on Pessah, Shavuot, and Sukkot. In the synagogue there is as well an עֲלִיָּה לַתּוֹרָה (*aliyah la-torah*), the "call to the reading of the Law." The Talmud records a very important rabbinic meeting concerning the limits of martyrdom that took place in an עֲלִיָּה (*aliyah*), "attic," the upper chamber of a house. And do you remember those old Egged buses struggling uphill? The bus's ability to climb is called its כֹּשֶׁר עֲלִיָּה (*kosher aliyah*).

What all of these usages have in common is the notion of ascension, from the root עלה (AYIN, LAMED, HEH), to "go up." It is not a coincidence that the national airline of Israel is called אֶל־עַל (*el al*), "to the heights." The verb עָלָה (*allah*) is used to express not only rising but costing, as in the question heard daily in Israel, כַּמָּה זֶה עוֹלֶה (*kammah zeh oleh*), "How much does this cost?"

One of the richest uses of the root is in its prepositional form עַל (*al*), used in a treasure trove of colorful expressions. When one engages in a debate, one of the tools one uses is the expression עַל אַחַת כַּמָּה וְכַמָּה (*al ahat kammah ve-khammah*), "How much more so." The Rabbis teach us לֹא עָלֶיךָ הַמְּלָאכָה לִגְמֹר (*lo alekha ha-melakhah ligmor*), "The important thing is to start a task, not necessarily to finish it." Cases in Jewish law are decided עַל פִּי שְׁנַיִם עֵדִים (*al pi shenayim edim*), "on the testimony of two witnesses." And let us not forget the edifying story of the Gentile who came to the sages Hillel and Shammai to learn the Torah עַל רֶגֶל אַחַת (al regel ahat), "standing on one foot." An issue you might want to discuss at your next meeting should be placed עַל הַפֶּרֶק (al ha-perek), "on the agenda." And when someone says to you תּוֹדָה (todah), "Thank you," the polite response is עַל לֹא דָבָר (al lo davar), "Think nothing of it."

A suggestion that all modern Israelis will consider מְעֻלֶּה (me'uleh), "outstanding," is to take the מַעֲלִית (ma'alit), elevator, to the קוֹמָה עֶלְיוֹנָה (komah elyonah), "top floor," for a breathtaking view. There you can also contemplate the story by I. L. Peretz, called in Hebrew אִם לֹא לְמַעֲלָה מִזֶּה (im lo le-ma'alah mi-zeh), "If Not Higher," in which doing a humble *mitsvah* is compared favorably with ascending to Heaven.

While neither of the two types of "American *aliyah*" is humble, it is always appropriate to weigh the benefits of each. The important thing, as always, is to begin.

60

עֲנָה

AYIN, NUN, HEH

THE BREADTH OF
AFFLICTION

That the Jews are a benevolent people is evident not only from their good works but also from their good wishes. They even wish each other well when they're not supposed to.

How else do you explain the greeting most often heard among American Jews on the day before Yom Kippur: "Have an easy fast." (In England and South Africa they say "Well over the fast," which is not as problematic.) How can you have an "easy" fast when the whole idea is to fulfill the biblical injunction — repeated four times in the Torah — וְעִנִּיתֶם אֶת נַפְשֹׁתֵיכֶם (ve-innitem et nafshoteikhem), "You shall afflict your souls." That affliction has to do with food is evident from the לֶחֶם עֹנִי (lehem oni), the "bread of affliction" our ancestors ate in Egypt. That the root עֲנָה (AYIN, NUN, HEH) means abstaining from food altogether is evident from the noun תַּעֲנִית (ta'anit), "fast."

The root has three meanings in addition to fasting: "to answer," "to chant," and, closest to the first meaning "to be poor or humble."

Something that requires a response is called in Hebrew an עִנְיָן (inyan), "a matter." One way to teach something מְעַנְיֵן (me'anyen), "interesting," about Jewish culture is to make use of the latest advances in information technology. In a lawsuit, you don't want somebody who is מְעֻנְיָן (me'unyan), "an interested party," to judge your case. When the congregation in the synagogue services expresses lyrical assent to a prayer, what it does is to עוֹנֶה אָמֵן (oneh amen), that is, it chants, in a time-honored melody, "amen."

A person who is fasting because he lacks the money to buy food is called an עָנִי (ani), a "pauper." A modest speaker will answer your question לְפִי עֲנִיּוּת דַעְתִּי (le-fi aniyut da'ati), "in my humble opinion."

Moses, our teacher, was the paradigmatic Jewish leader. He wasn't poor, but he wasn't proud either. In fact, the Torah praises him as an עָנָו (*anav*), a "humble man." We all know from experience that the passage from affliction to leadership does not always lead through humility. When it does, it is often recognizable as a Jewish way, or as Scripture puts it, עֵקֶב עֲנָוָה יִרְאַת ה' (*ekev anavah yirat ha-shem*), "In the footsteps of humility is the fear of God."

From this one might deduce that there is no such thing as an easy fast.

61

ערב

AYIN, RESH, VET

MIXING IT UP

You can tell a good deal about people from the way they divide their day. Not everyone counts by hours and minutes or day and night. Some think in terms of worktime and playtime; others relate only to mealtime and snacktime. The most venerable way of dividing the day, however, is recounted in the first chapter of Genesis: וַיְהִי עֶרֶב וַיְהִי בֹקֶר (va-yehi erev va-yehi voker), "There was evening, there was morning."

The etymology of the word עֶרֶב (erev) is curious, to say the least. It comes from the verb עָרַב (erav), "he mixed." Seen in this light, evening would be a mixture of daylight and darkness. The compounds of the three-letter root ערב (AYIN, RESH, VET) appear to be almost limitless, extending as they do to all areas of Jewish life. The west, where the sun sets, and therefore where evening begins, is called the מַעֲרָב (ma'arav). We all remember the poetic lament of Spanish-Jewish poet Yehuda ha-Levi, "My heart is in the east," וַאֲנֹכִי בְּסוֹף מַעֲרָב (va-anokhi be-sof ma'-arav), "but I am in the furthermost west." A similar-looking word, מַעֲרִיב (ma'ariv), is both the "evening prayer" and the name of Israel's evening newspaper.

In Jewish religious law, an עֵרוּב (eruv) is a device for mixing two pieces of property or two holy days so that one may carry on the Sabbath or cook for the Sabbath on a holy day. A person who mixes your interests with his so that you may do business more easily uses an עֵרָבוֹן (eravon), "pledge," to vouch for your credit. In Israel, a company בְּעֵרָבוֹן מֻגְבָּל (be-eravon mugbal) protects itself with "limited liability." This is abbreviated to בע״ם, like the British "Ltd." after a company's name.

You know of course that all Jews, closely knit together as they are, are responsible one for the other. In Hebrew (with an Aramaic tint) that comes out כָּל יִשְׂרָאֵל עֲרֵבִין זֶה בַּזֶּה (kol yisrael arevin zeh ba-zeh), "All Israel are intertwined."

In the Song of Songs, and in the repertoire of the late Jewish folk-

---

MIXING IT UP

singer Shlomo Carlebach, the poet entreats his beloved עֶרֶב הַשְׁמִיעֵנִי אֶת קוֹלֵךְ כִּי קוֹלֵךְ (hashmi'ini et kolekh ki kolekh arev), "Let me hear your voice for your voice is pleasant." How did the ערב root come to mean "pleasant"? Something that is עָרֵב (arev) is "mixed together well," one might say, wellseasoned and therefore pleasurable. A pleasant person in Hebrew is called מְעֹרָב עִם הַבְּרִיוֹת (me'orav im ha-beriyyiot), "mixed together with [God's] creatures."

Depending on the outcome, לְהִתְעָרֵב (le-hitarev), "to bet," can be pleasant or not. Would you like לְהִתְעָרֵב (le-hitarev) that the subject of chapter 9 is בֹּקֶר (boker), "morning"? Until then, עֶרֶב טוֹב (erev tov), "Have a good evening."

62

עֶרֶךְ

AYIN, RESH, KHAF

SEE UNDER: VALUE

A people's most precious possessions are often said to be the values by which it lives. In Jewish life, these values are known as עֲרָכִים (arakhim). The Hebrew root ערך (AYIN, RESH, KHAF) is particularly valuable because of the diversity of uses to which it is put.

The verb עָרַךְ (arakh) means "He arranged," "He set in order." In the Bible, it is found no fewer than twelve times coupled with the word מִלְחָמָה (milhamah), "war." To arrange in battle order and go to war is לַעֲרֹךְ מִלְחָמָה (la-arokh milhamah); a מַעֲרָכָה (ma'arakhah) would be the "battlefield" itself. A Jewish value of a completely different kind was posited in the sixteenth century when Rabbi Joseph Caro arranged the Jewish laws in order and called his codification the שׁוּלְחָן עָרוּךְ (shulhan arukh), literally, the "prepared table."

Nowadays, the root can be found not only on elegantly set dinner tables but in Israeli politics, where the מַעֲרָךְ (ma'arakh) is an "alignment" of like-thinking Laborite political parties. The root is also found in an Israeli child's schoolbag, where a מַעֲרֶכֶת (ma'arekhet) is a "schedule of classes"; in a museum, where a תַּעֲרוּכָה (ta'arukhah) is an "exhibit"; in the law courts, where an עוֹרֵךְ דִּין (orekh din) is a "lawyer"; and in the editorial offices of a newspaper, where an עוֹרֵךְ (orekh) is an "editor," the מַעֲרֶכֶת (ma'arekhet) is the "editorial staff," and עֲרִיכָה (arikhah) is the "editing" or "arranging" they do.

The noun עֶרֶךְ (erekh), "value," implies not only setting things beside one another but also judging their relative worth. In answer to your request for an opinion of a certain person, an Israeli may say, אֲנִי מַעֲרִיךְ אוֹתוֹ מְאֹד (ani ma'arikh oto me'od), "I esteem him greatly." As an adverb, the word בְּעֶרֶךְ (be-erekh) means "approximately." In conversational Hebrew it is sometimes used in the sense of the French expression "comme ci, comme ça." For example, in response to the question

מַה שְׁלוֹמְךָ (*mah shelomkha*), "How are you?" a laconic Israeli might answer בְּעֵרֶךְ (*be-erekh*), "Okay."

Words themselves are particularly precious in Hebrew. Every time
you look one up in a dictionary, you are looking up an עֵרֶךְ (*erekh*), a
"value," the Hebrew word meaning "dictionary entry." The English
term does not begin to convey the flavor of the Hebrew term. For example, the title of Israeli writer David Grossman's poignant novel
עַיֵן עֵרֶךְ: אַהֲבָה (*ayein erekh: ahavah*), "*See Under: Love*," plays on the word
"love" as both a dictionary entry and a value.

See under: Value.

63

עקב

AYIN, KOF, VET

FOOTSTEPS AND FOLLOW-UPS

Two gentlemen were sitting on a bench in Liberty Bell Park in Jerusalem. The older of the two, obviously a וָתִיק (*vatik*), "veteran," of many bureaucracy battles, was trying to explain to the recently arrived American how to deal successfully with Israeli bureaucrats.

(Astute readers cannot fail to have noticed that roots beginning with ו [VAV] are absent from our table of contents. Among the very few roots that have that peculiarity, like וו [VAV, VAV], "hook," and ותק [VAV, TAV, KOF], "seniority," none lends itself to an interesting treatment worthy of a complete chapter. It should nevertheless be considered a triumph of the author's astuteness to have been able to insert a couple of these roots here. Now back to our story.)

"The first 'no' doesn't count."

"Excuse me?"

"The first 'no' is designed to discourage frivolous petitioners who don't really need what they're asking for. If a person comes back after the first 'no,' then it's taken for granted that he's serious and he will be taken care of."

Mischievously, with a glint in his eye, the elderly gent switches to Hebrew. אַתָּה עוֹקֵב אַחֲרַי (*attah okev aharai*), "Do you follow me?"

The root of the verb לַעֲקֹב (*la-akov*) has a long and noble history. It is used here colloquially in an expression that pops out of the mouths of all types of professional explainers, from tour guides to teachers to bureaucrats. The root עקב (AYIN, KOF, VET) gives us the noun עָקֵב (*akev*), the "heel" of a foot. A popular tour in Israel takes participants בְּעִקְבוֹת הַנְּבִיאִים (*be-ikvot ha-nevi'im*), "in the footsteps of the prophets." The name of our forefather יַעֲקֹב (*ya'akov*) is said to derive from our root because, in utero, Jacob held on to the heel of his brother Esau to prevent him from passing first through the birth canal. Did Rabbi Akiva get his name from the same root? After all, when you walk, one heel follows the other, and so one who follows after God might well be called Akiva.

This type of speculation aside, a person who is עָקִיב (akiv) or, in more colloquial speech עִקְבִי (ikvi), "consistent," is so possibly because his opinions follow one another the way footprints resemble one another.

The root also implies causality. If your telephone service has been cut off, and you rush to a public phone to find out why, the voice on the other end of the wire will almost invariably answer עֵקֶב אִי־תַּשְׁלוּם (ekev i-tashlum), "because of nonpayment." In consequence, בְּעִקְבוֹת זֹאת (be-ikvot zot), you will be without a phone for a considerable length of time.

But don't despair, a מַעֲקָב (ma'akav), "follow-up," is always in order. Remember, the first "no" doesn't count.

64

פלג

FEH, LAMED, GIMMEL

WHO'S ARGUING?

The former Soviet Union refused to agree that the Jews had been singled out for destruction during the Holocaust. "Let's not divide the dead," they told Judith Miller, who reported on the subject in her book *One, By One, By One* (New York: Simon & Schuster, 1991). Unlike the Russians, the Jews are a nation that insists on dividing, especially when dividing means distinction making.

Take, for example, the Hebrew root פלג (FEH, LAMED, GIMMEL), "to cleave," "split," "divide." We find it in the Bible as a geographic descriptor. The place where the land is cleft to make room for a stream of water is called a פֶּלֶג (*peleg*). The Psalmist, in his very first chapter, compares the lover of God's Torah to an עֵץ שָׁתוּל עַל פַּלְגֵי מָיִם (*ets shatul al palgei mayim*), "a tree planted by a stream," a fruitful, prospering tree. This sense has entered into modern poetic Hebrew in the word פְּלַגְלַג (*pelaglag*), "brooklet," the sound of which onomatopoetically echoes the babbling of water.

For people tuned in to the sounds of words, babbling brooks always lead to the Tower of Babel. And were not those who engaged in its construction called by the Rabbis the דוֹר הַפְּלַגָּה (*dor ha-pelagah*), "the schismatic generation"? The word פְּלֻגְתָּא (*pelugta*), "talmudic debate," has given rise to an Aramaic phrase in modern Hebrew, לֵית מָאן דְּפָלִיג (*let man de-palig*), roughly translated as "Who's arguing?"

To be sure, the Rabbis were well aware of the positive effects of dividing. In the *Nishmat* prayer recited on *Shabbat* and holiday mornings, we assert to God that אֵבָרִים שֶׁפִּלַּגְתָּ בָּנוּ (*evarim she-pilagta banu*), "The very limbs that You have 'divvied out' to us," shall praise You.

The coiners of modern Hebrew had genial successes with this root. They were right on the mark when they termed a political party a מִפְלָגָה (*miflagah*). Did they see that it would be the proliferation of political parties in Israel that would divide the country and give the Jew-

---

ish people a chronic פָּלֶג (*poleg*), a "migraine headache" (because, as the French word *migraine* suggests, it divides the cranium in half)?

The root is used today in both war and peace. In army lingo a פְּלֻגָּה (*pelugah*) is a "division" of soldiers. On a pleasant day in the Bay of Haifa one can see more than one pleasure boat as it מַפְלִיג (*maflig*), "sets sail," that is, "separates" itself from the shore. Separation, as thousands of new Israelis from the former Soviet Union will now attest, can often be a pleasure. And dividing the dead may be precisely the right thing to do.

65

פלל

FEH, LAMED, LAMED

GOOD JUDGMENT

One of the first lessons they teach you in translators' school is that there are no exact equivalents. Especially when going from one language family to another – for example, from Romance to Slavic, or from Germanic to Semitic – what you get is, at best, a dazzling approximation and, at worst, a dismal betrayal of meaning. The problem is compounded when you go from one cultural polarity to another.

Take the example of prayer. The English verb "to pray" has its roots in the Romance languages. One can see the family relationship in, for example, the Italian *pregare* and the French *prier*. There, as in English, the verb means simply "to beg," "to beseech," "to entreat." What does this have to do with the Hebrew word for prayer, תְּפִלָּה (*tefillah*)? Virtually nothing.

Chaim Rabin, a historian of the Hebrew language, tells us that between the third and the eighth centuries our playful *Payyetanim*, composers of liturgical poetry, invented thousands of Hebrew words, among them the word מִפְלָל (*miflal*), a play on our word for prayer that emphasizes its root, פלל (FEH, LAMED, LAMED). The root of the Hebrew noun תְּפִלָּה (*tefillah*) can also be found in the Hebrew infinitive for "to pray," לְהִתְפַּלֵּל (*le-hitpallel*). Why this verb is in the reflexive form will be examined soon. Originally, the verb לְפַלֵּל (*le-fallel*) meant "to think." When Jacob is on his deathbed in Egypt, after having reencountered his newly powerful son, he says to Joseph רְאֹה פָנֶיךָ לֹא פִלָּלְתִּי (*re'o fanekha lo fillalti*), "I did not think I would ever see your face again" (Genesis 48:11).

Since thinking implies judgment, the root has been used with that connotation as well. A פָּלִיל (*palil*) in antiquity was a "judge" and a פְּלִילָה (*pelilah*), a "judgment." Often these judgments have to do with criminal cases, as evidenced by the expressions בֵּית דִּין פְּלִילִי (*bet din pelili*), "criminal court," and פְּלִילִיּוּת (*peliliyut*), "criminality" in general.

From this survey, we may conclude that the verb לְהִתְפַּלֵּל (le-hitpallel), in the reflexive, does not mean "to pray" in the sense of "to entreat" but rather "to judge one's own actions" and, often, to find oneself in need of judgment.

In Philip Roth's masterpiece, the novel *The Counterlife* (New York: Farrar, Straus and Giroux, 1986), Nathan Zuckerman finds himself at the Western Wall. Although he takes an interest in his fellow Jews at prayer, he refuses all invitations to pray. Prayer, in the sense of begging, he insists, is beneath his dignity. And yet, it is ironic that Roth's heroes are constantly judging themselves, engaged perhaps in the higher sense of תְּפִלָּה (tefillah). Might one not conclude that Philip Roth, the anatomist of Jewish guilt, is therefore a בַּעַל תְּפִלָּה (ba'al tefillah), "prayer leader," of the Jewish people? But then again, there are no exact equivalents.

66

פנה

FEH, NUN, HEH

TURNING THE OTHER FACE

Different cultures often have different words to describe the same phenomenon. In the United States, Jewish organizations have recently begun to deal with a social group known as "singles," offering them, as inducements to change their status to "married," a full panoply of programs, from singles *minyanim* to singles bike trips.

In Israel, these unmarried folk are not known as "singles" but as פְּנוּיִים (*penuyim*, masculine) and פְּנוּיוֹת (*penuyot*, feminine), "availables." It is not coincidental that the Hebrew term connotes a readiness to change one's status.

The word פְּנוּיִים (*penuyim*), prevalent in current usage, goes back to rabbinic Hebrew and to the Rabbis' discussions of all sorts of issues between the sexes. The root goes back even further, to the verb פָּנָה (*panah*), which has in it the sense of "turning" necessary for a change in status. From that root we get such diverse terms as פַּן (*pan*), a "facet" of a geometric figure revealed as the latter turns; פָּנִים (*panim*), "face," perhaps because we turn to face each other; פִּנָּה (*pinnah*), "corner," because that's what walkers turn; and the idiom לִפְנוֹת בֹּקֶר (*lifnot boker*), "before dawn," because that's when night turns into day.

The singular forms of our adjective, פָּנוּי (*panui*) and פְּנוּיָה (*penuyah*), have many uses in modern Hebrew. If you need a place to live, you look for a דִּירָה פְּנוּיָה (*dirah penuyah*), a "vacant apartment"; to earn a living, you look in the want ads for a מִשְׂרָה פְּנוּיָה (*misrah penuyah*), a "position available."

One of the most important national concerns of the Israeli government is how best to occupy the שְׁעוֹת הַפְּנַאי (*sha'ot ha-penai*), "leisure time," of its citizens. One of the more worthy leisure-time activities is adult study. The Rabbis of *Pirkei Avot* (Ethics of the Fathers) thought so too, but they knew that leisure means different things to different people, saying אַל תֹּאמַר לִכְשֶׁאֶפָּנֶה אֶשְׁנֶה שֶׁמָּא לֹא תִּפָּנֶה (*al tomar likhshe-efneh esh-*

neh shema lo tipaneh), "Do not say, 'When I shall have leisure, I shall study'; perhaps you won't have leisure."

Did you realize that the English word "vacation" is related to "vacancy" and that both are related to "evacuation"? In Hebrew, too. When the town of Yamit was evacuated to make way for peace with Egypt, Yamit's residents were known as מְפֻנֵי יָמִית (*mufnei yamit*), "Yamit's evacuees." Even in Jerusalem, if you don't pay your rent, you can find a צַו פִּינוּי (*tsav pinui*), "evacuation notice," tacked on your door. The clerk in the office where you go to complain about this injustice will use the verb לְהַפְנוֹת (*le-hafnot*) to "refer" you to someone who can handle your problem.

Will the problem be handled to your satisfaction? That depends on who is פָּנוּי (*panui*), "available," to speak with you פָּנִים אֶל פָּנִים (*panim el panim*), "face to face," to settle your case.

67

פסק

FEH, SAMEKH, KOF

STOP IN THE NAME OF THE
LORE

Classical Jewish literature comes in two flavors – legal debate and fanciful story – and the Rabbis were adept at both. When they liked a particular story, the Rabbis told it over and over again, changing only the details of the narrative to suit their message. Such is the case with the several rabbinic tales whose fulcrum is the statement פְּסוֹק לִי פְּסוּקֵיךָ (*pesok li pesukekha*), "Recite to me your [recently learned] verses."

It seems that, whenever a character in a rabbinic tale (whether Purim hero Mordecai or apostate Elisha ben Abuya) had need of a parable from which to learn his fate, he would seek out schoolboys and ask them what biblical verse they had learned that day. The schoolchildren, who were believed to have oracular powers, would recite a פָּסוּק (*pasuk*), "verse," called for by the context of the hero's predicament.

The noun פָּסוּק (*pasuk*) comes from the root פסק (FEH, SAMEKH, KOF), which originally meant "to discontinue," "to stop." Thus, הַגְּשָׁמִים פָּסְקוּ (*ha-geshamim pasku*) signifies that "the rain has stopped." The סְעוּדָה הַמַּפְסֶקֶת (*se'udah ha-mafseket*) is the meal after which one stops eating before Yom Kippur. A פָּסוּק (*pasuk*), a "biblical verse," is created when it stops. Note that a פָּסוּק (*pasuk*) is not necessarily a sentence. According to one translation of the Torah, the first sentence of Genesis is made up of its first three פְּסוּקִים (*pesukim*).

The generic term for stopping is הֶפְסֵק (*hefsek*), "discontinuity." The specific term is הַפְסָקָה (*hafsakah*), usually denoting an "intermission" at the theater or a "recess" at school. The modern way of taking a "time-out" on an Israeli soccer field is to ask for a פֶּסֶק זְמָן (*pesek zeman*). If you ask for a פֶּסֶק זְמָן (*pesek zeman*) at a snack shop, you'll be given a candy bar with that brand name.

The root is also used in פִּסּוּק (*pissuk*), Hebrew "punctuation." In the synagogue service, the Torah is chanted according to a system of musical notation. Each note has a specific sound, except the פְּסִיק (*pesik*), which tells the Torah reader to pause between two words. In modern Hebrew, a פְּסִיק (*pesik*) is also a pause, and looks very much like the punctuation mark between the words "pause" and "and" in this sentence, that is, a "comma." A period is, not surprisingly, a סוֹף פָּסוּק (*sof pasuk*), an "end stop." A group of sentences built around a single idea is called a פִּסְקָה (*piskah*), "paragraph."

How is the root פסק (FEH, SAMEKH, KOF) related to the noun פּוֹסֵק (*posek*), "religious decisor"? A legal discussion is ended when someone with the authority to do so, called a פּוֹסֵק (*posek*), stops all debate and renders a verdict.

Sometimes legal debates, fanciful stories, and chapters about Hebrew roots come to an end at precisely the right moment. Let's stop here, therefore, with an elegant סוֹף פָּסוּק (*sof pasuk*).

68

פקד

FEH, KOF, DALET

TASK MASTERS

Have you ever asked yourself why the fourth fifth of the Penta-teuch, called in Hebrew בְּמִדְבַּר (*be-midbar*), is called "Numbers" in English? The answer is found in the Talmud, which calls this book חוּמָשׁ הַפִּקּוּדִים (*humash ha-pikkudim*), the "numbering fifth." It is an apt description, since the root פקד (FEH, KOF, DALET), "to number," appears in the Book of Numbers alone more than one hundred times.

In truth, the root has several meanings, not all of them obviously related. The verb פָּקַד (*pakad*), for example, can mean things as seemingly disconnected as "to count," "to muster" the troops, "to give orders," "to remember" for both evil and good, "to visit," and, by extension and by euphemism, "to have sexual relations."

To begin with, Genesis relates that God פָּקַד (*pakad*), "remembered," Sarah and His promise that she would bear children. Let's continue with the relationship between counting and commanding. It is clear from both Numbers and Samuel that the object of a census in the Bible is the preparation of a register of all men capable of bearing arms. You count in order to assess military strength. Thus, a מִפְקָד (*mifkad*) is a "census," while a מְפַקֵּד (*mefakked*) is a "military commander." A newspaper story out of Israel might tell us that הַקְרָב הִתְנַהֵל בְּפִקּוּדוֹ שֶׁל הָאַלּוּף (*ha-kerav hitnahel be-fikkudo shel ha-aluf*), "The battle was fought under the command of the brigadier general." Once the soldiers have been told לְהִתְפַּקֵּד (*le-hitpakked*), "Sound off!" at the מִפְקָד (*mifkad*), "muster," it is very efficient for the officer to hand out the various תַּפְקִידִים (*tafkidim*), "assignments," and to give the soldiers their פְּקוּדּוֹת (*pekuddot*), "orders."

From the battlefield, let's go to the office and the bank (a linguistic military-industrial complex, if ever there was one). If a פָּקִיד (*pakid*) in biblical Hebrew is an "officer," in modern Hebrew it is a "bureaucrat,"

---

someone who works in an office; פְּקִידוּת (*pekidut*) is both the work done there and the clerical staff.

In Jewish law, a thing for which one assumes responsibility is called a פִּקָּדוֹן (*pikkadon*). One of the first legal cases a Talmud student learns is הַמַּפְקִיד (*ha-mafkid*), dealing with a situation where one person gives another responsibility for his property. Today, that is precisely what you do when you make a פִּקָּדוֹן (*pikkadon*), a "deposit," in the bank.

Another meaning of לִפְקֹד (*lifkod*) is "to visit." The Talmud – ever realistic – uses this verb to remind us that a husband is obligated to "visit" his wife before a long journey.

The euphemism leads not only to memories but also to generations that can be counted.

69

פרס

FEH, RESH, SAMEKH

WELL–KNOWN MIRACLES

It is well known that the holiday of Hanukkah celebrates the victory of the Hebraists over the Hellenizers. We light candles to commemorate the Temple miracle that accompanied this moral victory.

Ironically, the Aramaic expression used by the Rabbis as the halakhic rationale for kindling the Hanukkah lights — פַּרְסוּמֵי נִסָּא (*parsumei nissa*), "to publicize the miracle" — is itself, according to some scholars, of Greek origin. The four-letter Hebrew root פרסם (FEH, RESH, SAMEKH, MEM) would come from the same Greek source that gives us the Aramaic expression בְּפַרְהֶסְיָה (*be-farhesiah*), "in public." The letter מ (MEM) was simply added to form the Hebrew verb פִּרְסֵם (*pirsem*), "He made public." Not satisfied with this problematic explanation, involving, as it does, added letters, other scholars have suggested that our root comes from the three-letter Hebrew root פרס (FEH, RESH, SAMEKH), "to spread." The problem here is that these scholars also have to add a מ (MEM) to make up the four-letter Hebrew root. A plausible argument in favor of a Greek origin is that the verb פִּרְסֵם (*pirsem*) is found nowhere in the Hebrew Bible.

It is, however, found abundantly in rabbinic literature, in a series of usages that mirror the Rabbis' value system. According to the Rabbis, scholars should be modest about their learning; when they are supposed to be מְפוּרְסָמִים (*mefursamim*), "well known," it is not by their learning but by their good deeds.

The past participle מְפוּרְסָם (*mefursam*), "well known," is found in modern Hebrew as well, for example in the expression הַמְשׁוֹרֵר הַמְפוּרְסָם (*ha-meshorer ha-mefursam*), "the well-known poet." Of course, if the poet's agent has engaged in the appropriate פִּרְסֹמֶת (*pirsomet*), "publicity," and if the poet and his פִּרְסוּמִים (*pirsumim*), "publications," are really well known, you shouldn't have to say so.

In a recent poem, the well known Israeli poet Yehuda Amichai wrote, "Languages are like cats / One must not go against the direction of the fur" (translation by Robert Alter). Hanukkah reminds us that Hebrew and Greek go in different directions. As the example of our root demonstrates, however, Jewish users of Hebrew can't seem to resist the temptation to make Greek and other Western languages take a Jewish direction.

That they succeed so often is perhaps another miracle that requires פַּרְסוּמֵי נִסָּא (*parsumei nissa*).

70

פרש

FEH, RESH, SHIN

APART TOGETHER

In the United States, as in other parts of the Jewish world, the Hebrew term פָּרָשַׁת הַשָּׁבוּעַ (*parashat ha-shavu'a*) has a distinctly religious flavor. It refers to the weekly Torah portion read in the synagogue on *Shabbat*.

This is not exclusively the case in Israel. In the Holy Land, the Holy Tongue has been successfully integrated into everyday speech. Thus we have a secular language laden with religious allusions. For example, during the briefest of bus rides in Jerusalem, one can overhear Israelis giving a new meaning to פָּרָשַׁת הַשָּׁבוּעַ (*parashat ha-shavu'a*), "the weekly portion." Buzzing through the air is talk of all the different פָּרָשׁוֹת (*parashot*), "affairs" or "scandals," that seem to pop up weekly in Israel.

The noun פָּרָשָׁה (*parashah*) comes from the root פרש (FEH, RESH, SHIN), "to distinguish." The infinitive לִפְרֹשׁ (*lifrosh*) means "to divide" an ongoing story into its constituent chapters or parts. When you take a closer look at one of these parts in order to give it an interpretation, you are engaged in the hallowed Jewish occupation of פַּרְשָׁנוּת (*par-shanut*), "commentary." One engaged in providing a text with a פֵּרוּשׁ (*perush*), "interpretation," is called a פַּרְשָׁן (*parshan*), "commentator" or "exegete."

In another verb form, the root means to set aside. There are some people who still remember when their grandmother would, during the baking of חַלּוֹת (*hallot*), "Sabbath loaves," set aside some of the dough for ritual purposes. The blessing she would make would end with the words לְהַפְרִישׁ חַלָּה (*le-hafrish hallah*), "to set aside a portion."

The root also contains the sense of crossing. The place where a road separates into various branches is called a פָּרָשַׁת דְּרָכִים (*parashat derakhim*), a "crossroads." Someone who has to decide "where to go from here" is said to be, figuratively, עַל פָּרָשַׁת דְּרָכִים (*al parashat der-*

akhim). According to Zionist thinker Ahad Ha-am, in a major essay of the same name, that is where the Jewish people found themselves before the founding of the State. Once a choice has been indicated בִּמְפוֹרָשׁ (*bimforash*), "explicitly," then we know how to resume our way.

Modern rabbinic Judaism stems from a large sect of Jews — the פְּרוּשִׁים (*perushim*), "Pharisees" — who set themselves apart from those who would not recognize the primacy of the Oral Law. Obviously, not all setting apart is good. A united Jewish community is such a strong Jewish value that the Rabbis had a proverb for it: אַל תִּפְרוֹשׁ מִן הַצִּבּוּר (*al tifrosh min ha-tsibbur*), "Do not separate yourself from the community."

The weekly פָּרָשָׁה (*parashah*) is a division that both sets us apart and keeps us together.

71

פשט

FEH, SHIN, TET

A SIMPLE STORY

Contrary to popular belief, Hebrew is not a difficult language. Think of all the third-graders in Israel who speak it fluently. Then again, Hebrew is not a simple language either. Think, for example, of the Hebrew word for "simple," פָּשׁוּט (pashut).

When Nobel Prize winner S. Y. Agnon's novel סִפּוּר פָּשׁוּט (sippur pashut), A Simple Story, was published in English by Schocken Books, readers and reviewers alike were puzzled. The story, yet another tale of a traditional Jew's confrontation with modernity, was anything but simple. An ingenious explanation was suggested by an Israeli linguist who noted that one of the meanings of the root פשט (FEH, SHIN, TET) is "widespread." Agnon was simply retelling a popular, well-known story.

How are פָּשׁוּט (pashut), "simple," and פָּשׁוּט (pashut), "spread out," related? The relationship is similar to the two meanings of the English word "plain." As an adjective, "plain" is simple. As a noun, a "plain" is an extensive area. The meaning of a word, its פְּשָׁט (peshat), is also its "explanation." To explain is to make plain.

It is obvious, or as the Rabbis say in Aramaic, פְּשִׁיטָא (peshita), that the source of our root is in the Torah. There, however, the root means "to remove," "to take off." When a serpent פּוֹשֵׁט אֶת הָעוֹר (poshet et ha-or), "sheds its skin," the skin flattens out and loses its rounded contour. From serpents to human beings is but a short step, as seen from the verb לְהִתְפַּשֵּׁט (le-hitpashet), "to get undressed."

The serpent has neither feet nor hands, but the verb פּוֹשֵׁט (poshet), "He stretches," has both. Of a businessperson who has extended himself too far, it is said that he פָּשַׁט אֶת הָרֶגֶל (pashat et ha-regel), literally, "He has stretched his leg," figuratively, "He has gone bankrupt." It is understood that one who פּוֹשֵׁט יָד (poshet yad), "stretches forth his hand," is asking for alms. Perhaps there is a relation between these two uses of the same verb, a causal one.

The root, further, is used in both concrete and abstract situations. "Abstract thinking" is in Hebrew מַחֲשָׁבָה מוּפְשֶׁטֶת (*mahshavah mufshetet*). Why so? Again, think of the English word "abstract." It originally meant "stretched out" but today is often applied to an idea that is difficult to understand.

That's how something פָּשׁוּט (*pashut*), "plain," and something מֻפְשָׁט (*mufshat*), "abstract," can be both simple and difficult at the same time. Just like Hebrew.

72

צנע

TSADI, NUN, AYIN

A MODESTY PROPOSAL

Jewish values can be found in the most surprising places. If, for example, it is your custom to visit the cemetery during the days preceding Yom Kippur, you might want to make an effort to look especially closely at the tombstones of pious Jewish women buried there. You will find that the praise most frequently engraved in Hebrew on women's monuments is the expression אִשָּׁה צְנוּעָה (*ishah tsenu'ah*), "a modest woman." One might say that there are sermons in these stones. In the Hebrew root צנע (TSADI, NUN, AYIN), "to conceal," "to be modest," you will also find other verbal treasures.

The root appears only twice in the Bible, but it appears in an expression that has attained great vogue in polite English. The admonition to "do justly, love mercy, and walk humbly with your God" comes from the prophet Micah's Hebrew, where the last part — "walk humbly with your God" — is rendered using our root: הַצְנֵעַ לֶכֶת עִם אֱלֹקֶיךָ (*hatsne'a lekhet im elokekha*). The Book of Proverbs, containing Judaism's quintessential wisdom, teaches that צְנוּעִים חָכְמָה (*tsenu'im hokhmah*), "with the lowly is found wisdom."

The original meaning of the root, that of hiding or concealment, is used extensively in rabbinic Hebrew. Intriguingly, we learn that while all other *mitsvot* were given publicly, the *Shabbat* was given to the Jews as a private *mitsvah*. The root is used in rabbinic literature in connection with the notion of saving money, לְהַצְנִיעַ (*le-hatsni'a*), "to put aside," "to withdraw from circulation." To withdraw a person from circulation — a mild form of excommunication — is also לְהַצְנִיעַ (*le-hatsni'a*) that person.

Undoubtedly the most popular use of the root is the word צְנִיעוּת (*tseni'ut*), "modesty." There is a form of צְנִיעוּת (*tseni'ut*) that has to do with high necklines and long sleeves; then there is the more spiritual צְנִיעוּת (*tseni'ut*) that has everything to do with one's philosophical outlook on life. More properly translated as "meekness," this form of צְנִיעוּת (*tseni'ut*) has to do with the way you perceive your place in the world in relation to the vastness of the universe.

Today, Israel's economy is better than it has ever been. During the years immediately following the founding of the State, however, there was a period when all sorts of goods were in short supply; this was known as the תְּקוּפַת הַצֶּנַע (*tekufat ha-tsena*), the "era of austerity." It was a period when people took pride in "making do." It also gave rise to a Hebrew slang equivalent of the Yiddish-American term "shlock." If, for example, you wanted to point to cheap furniture of poor quality, you would speak of רְהִיטֵי צֶנַע (*rehitei tsena*).

Nowadays, Israel may indeed have a little צֶנַע (*tsena*) of that type, but there are still plenty of אֲנָשִׁים צְנוּעִים (*anashim tsenu'im*), "unpretentious, decorous human beings," there to make it all worthwhile.

73

צפן

TSADI, FEH, NUN

HIDDEN TREASURES

"Search me, a treasure is hidden inside." This phrase, taken from the *Fables* of French author Jean de la Fontaine, is meant to teach us the intrinsic worth of even the most familiar object, unassuming person, or humble word. Take, for example, the Hebrew word צָפַן (*tsafan*), "He has hidden," and you will find all sorts of cultural treasures hidden inside.

In the Torah, the root צפן (TSADI, FEH, NUN) occurs first in Genesis, where the Jewish people are promised that they will spread abroad in the four directions of the compass. The northern direction is called צָפוֹן (*tsafon*), presumably because when the sun is not visible, it is "hiding" in the north. The root is also used in connection with the infant Moses, who was hidden from Pharaoh by his mother, Yokheved, for three months: וַתִּצְפְּנֵהוּ (*va-titspeneihu*), "She hid him." According to tradition, Joseph was given the name צָפְנַת פַּעְנֵחַ (*tsofnat pa'ne'ah*) by *his* Pharaoh because, as an interpreter of dreams, Joseph was talented in revealing hidden things. Then there is the prophet צְפַנְיָה (*tsefaniah*), whose name means "whom God has treasured."

In the Passover *Haggadah*, the word צָפוּן (*tsafun*) is prominent. This is the name of the eleventh of fourteen tasks to be performed during the Seder. It refers to the eating of the *afikoman*, the piece of *matsah* that had been hidden just prior to the festive meal.

Whether you go north, south, east, or west, you would do well to take along a מַצְפֵּן (*matspen*), "compass." Incidentally, this was the name of a small New Left political party that existed in Israel during the 1960s. Their compass called for withdrawal from the territories immediately after the Six Day War.

Colloquial Hebrew is adept at assimilating idioms whole from other languages. Thus the French slang expression *perdre le nord*, literally, "to lose the north," figuratively, "to become confused," has made

---

its way into modern Hebrew as לְאַבֵּד אֶת הַצָּפוֹן (le-abbed et ha-tsafon), "to lose one's bearings."

In the espionage dodge, it is often necessary to use a hidden language; that is why the secret services will use a צֹפֶן (tsofen), "code." The hidden place where the motives for our behavior are comfortably concealed is called the מַצְפּוּן (matspun), "conscience." In democratic societies like Israel and the United States, one of the basic freedoms is חֹפֶשׁ הַמַּצְפּוּן (hofesh ha-matspun), "freedom of conscience."

Obviously, democracies, which posit the goodness of humankind, believe that what is hidden inside the mind can also be a treasure.

74

צרך

TSADI, RESH, KHAF

THE MOTHER OF NECESSITY

Necessity, they say, is the mother of invention. In Jewish culture, however, necessity is often used as an instrument of conciliation, as a means for seeing the cosmic harmony of the universe. A typical talmudic sequence will ask, for example, "Why do we require verse 'y' when we already have verse 'x,' which says substantially the same thing?" Almost inevitably the talmudic response is צְרִיכָא (tserikha), "It is necessary." Why? To fulfill some other equally important purpose of the law.

The root צרך (TSADI, RESH, KHAF) appears only once in Scripture (in what is called, you will recall from an earlier chapter, a *hapax legomenon*) in Second Chronicles, in a letter from the king of Tyre to King Solomon offering to send him cedar from Lebanon כְּכָל צָרְכֶּךְ (ke-khol tsorkekha), "as much as you will need" for the building of the Temple.

The root finds its way into rabbinic literature not only in talmudic discourse but also in liturgical texts, especially in those with an ethical dimension. The *Haggadah* provides us with a formula for inviting כָּל דִצְרִיךְ (kol ditsrikh), "all who are in need," to partake of the festival meal. And in the Sabbath service there is a special blessing for those who occupy themselves with צָרְכֵי צִבּוּר (tsorkhei tsibbur), "the needs of the community."

In both rabbinic and modern Hebrew the verb צָרִיךְ (tsarikh) is used in much the same way that *il faut*, "It is necessary," is used in French. A quaint expression with a gallic touch of gallantry is צָרִיךְ אָדָם לְהַחֲנִיף לְאִשְׁתּוֹ (tsarikh adam le-hahanif le-ishto), "A man must flatter his wife."

In modern Hebrew, the root is found in situations dealing with the purchase of commodities. Every nation needs to know, for example, what its תִּצְרֹכֶת דֶּלֶק (titsrokhet delek), "fuel consumption," is. It is telling, is it not, that a speaker of English who buys goods is called a "consumer," while in Hebrew a consumer is called a צַרְכָן (tsarkhan), a "needer." The most famous department store in Israel is called הַמַּשְׁבִּיר

לַצַּרְכָן (ha-mashbir la-tsarkhan), "the provider to the consumer." A cooperative store run by the workers of a large hospital would be called a צַרְכָנִיָּה (tsarkhaniyyah) and the "necessities" one would buy there are called מִצְרָכִים (mitsrakhim).

It is curious that the reflexive form of the verb לְהִצְטָרֵךְ (le-hit-starekh) has a ט (TET) instead of the usual ת (TAV) as a sign of the reflexive. Why this is so is known, of course, to grammarians.

We will content ourselves with the pithy Hebrew expression צָרִיךְ עִיּוּן (tsarikh iyyun), "It requires further study."

75

קדש

KOF, DALET, SHIN

HOLY, HOLY, HOLY

The first word Jews pronounce at the Passover Seder is the programmatic announcement קַדֵּשׁ (*kaddesh*), literally, "Sanctify," practically, "Make the blessing over the wine." With that word, even before we perform the act itself, we leave the world of the everyday and enter into the realm of redemption. Where does the power of this three-letter word come from? From its meaning, to be sure, but most importantly, from the uses to which its meaning has been put.

Originally, the root קדש (KOF, DALET, SHIN) possessed the idea of separation, of setting aside for a specific use. That's the way it has been used in the evening ritual of קִדּוּשׁ (*kiddush*), with which we begin *Shabbat* as well as Pessah, Shavuot, Sukkot, and Rosh Hashana. The *Shabbat* morning *kiddush* in synagogue – at which an overabundance of food is normally served – seems to have been designed to separate the weekday protein intake from *Shabbat's* ingestion of carbohydrates.

In biblical times, the root had cultic uses, and not only among the Israelites. Pagan practice used to set aside a קָדֵשׁ (*kadesh*) or a קְדֵשָׁה (*kedeshah*) as a temple prostitute in the service of, among others, the goddess Astarte. Israelite religion, of course, abominated this practice but did not, for all that, disdain the Semitic root. The Holy Temple itself is, after all, called the בֵּית הַמִּקְדָּשׁ (*beit ha-mikdash*). And Hebrew and Arabic both use the same Semitic root to call Jerusalem the "City of Holiness" – in Hebrew עִיר הַקּוֹדֶשׁ (*ir ha-kodesh*) and in Arabic *Al Quds*.

Not surprisingly, the word is found in Jewish life-cycle events. The marriage formula recited by the groom is הֲרֵי אַתְּ מְקֻדֶּשֶׁת לִי (*harei at mekudeshet li*), "Behold, you are sanctified to me." The prayer recited by mourners is not a prayer for the dead but rather the קַדִּישׁ (*kaddish*), an affirmation of the sanctity of God.

Modern usage has contributed to the secularization – in the good

---

sense – of the word. A hotel for poor people set up by the community was called a הֶקְדֵּשׁ (*hekdesh*); Yiddish speakers, aware that these places tend to be untidy, took to calling any messy room a הֶקְדֵּשׁ (*hekdesh*). The dedication of a book in modern-day Israel is called a הַקְדָּשָׁה (*hakdashah*). The traditional expression for Jewish martyrdom is קִדּוּשׁ הַשֵּׁם (*kiddush ha-shem*), "sanctification of the Name." Today, any righteous action by a Jew that makes the Jews look good in the eyes of the world is also called a קִדּוּשׁ הַשֵּׁם (*kiddush ha-shem*).

For the second word pronounced at the Passover *Seder*, please see your *Haggadah*.

76

קהל

KOF, HEH, LAMED

A GATHERING OF JEWS

With rare exceptions, traditional Jewish women are exempt from performing, as the Rabbis put it, "positive commandments that are time-bound." One of these exceptions is Jewish study. How is Jewish study time-bound, you may ask? We are all aware that once every seven years the Jews who work the Land of Israel observe a sabbatical year, שְׁמִטָּה (shemittah), and, theoretically at least, let the land lie fallow. It appears that to inaugurate the eighth year, according to Deuteronomy 31:10–13, all Jews — men, women, and children — gather together in Jerusalem on the first day of Sukkot in a festival known as יוֹם הַקְהֵל (yom hak'hel), a "Day of Gathering," to listen to a reading of the Book of Deuteronomy and to study it.

The word הַקְהֵל (hak'hel), although used as a noun in rabbinic parlance when discussing the holiday, is not a noun but a causative verb in the imperative meaning "Cause [the Children of Israel] to gather." It comes from the root קהל (KOF, HEH, LAMED), "to assemble," "to gather."

The root appears most prominently in Scripture in the Hebrew name of one of the most important texts of Judaism's "Wisdom Literature," the Book of Ecclesiastes, קֹהֶלֶת (kohelet). In the opinion of some, the word designated some kind of "officer." Since the authorship of the book is ascribed to King Solomon, others say that he was given the name קֹהֶלֶת (kohelet) because, as king, he was "one who assembles a congregation." Rashi, commenting on the first verse of the scroll, puts it a bit more imaginatively: Solomon is called Kohelet because "he gathers all wisdom unto himself."

Whether gathering wisdom or Jews, the root קהל (KOF, HEH, LAMED) is associated with several Jewish institutions and is found today in religious, political, and cultural Jewish contexts.

Since one of the meanings of the noun קָהָל (kahal) is "congregation," it should not be surprising to find it as part of the name of synagogues, as, for example, קְהַל עֲדַת יְשׁוּרוּן (*kehal adat yeshurun*), "Congregation Adath Yeshurun," founded in Frankfurt, Germany.

In modern idiomatic Hebrew a קְהִלִּיָּה (*kehilliyyah*) is a "republic" or "commonwealth." More important for American Jewish history was the short-lived New York קְהִלָּה (*kehillah*) founded in 1909 by Judah Magnes, which, for a dozen years, more or less successfully "governed" New York City's Jews.

If you get your Jewish kicks not from politics but from Jewish culture, you might want to think about joining your community's מַקְהֵלָה (*mak'helah*), "choir," a community of singers.

Some people think that at the root of our root is a word that stems from קוֹל (KOF, VAV, LAMED), "to call by voice to an assembly." Whether or not this is so, it appears that Jewish דַּעַת־קָהָל (*da'at kahal*), "public opinion," is determined that all Jews be included in the call.

77

קוֹם

KOF, VAV, MEM

TAKING A STAND

A Jerusalem story. Two American teenagers living in the capital are strolling one evening in Independence Park when they are approached by a border policeman who is himself obviously from out of town. When told "We live in Talbieh," he looks suspiciously and in vain at his map of Jerusalem for the neighborhood bearing that Arabic name. Tension mounts for the two teens – his Jeep's spotlight shining in their eyes – until a colleague comes to clear up the matter. "The neighborhood called Talbieh by everyone," he explains, "is קוֹמְמִיּוּת (*kommemiyut*) in Hebrew, chosen because it means sovereignty and independence. Why, it was even one of the names once considered for the new Jewish State."

The word קוֹמְמִיּוּת (*kommemiyut*), "standing up straight," is derived from the noun קוֹמָה (*komah*), "height" or "stature." It also denotes the story of a building, as in הַקּוֹמָה הַשְּׁלִישִׁית (*ha-komah ha-shelishit*), "the third floor." Both קוֹמָה (*komah*) and קוֹמְמִיּוּת (*kommemiyut*), as well as, surprisingly enough, the noun for place, מָקוֹם (*makom*), come from the three-letter root קוֹם (KOF, VAV, MEM), "to stand up." The root has almost a dozen other related senses, including "to establish." One of the most frequently heard expressions in Israeli political discourse is לִפְנֵי קוֹם הַמְּדִינָה (*lifnei kom ha-medinah*), "before the establishment of the State."

It is fascinating to observe in how many expressions relating to ethical behavior the root is found. One of the most beautiful of these is נָאֶה דוֹרֵשׁ וְנָאֶה מְקַיֵּם (*na'eh doresh ve-na'eh mekayyem*), used to praise someone both for fulfilling his or her promises and for asking of oneself no less than one asks of others. Both the holiness code of Leviticus and the Egged Bus Company teach us the Jewish value of respect for the elderly in the expression מִפְּנֵי שֵׂיבָה תָּקוּם (*mipnei seivah takum*), "You shall rise before the hoary head" (and give your seat on the bus to a senior citizen). And what about those little toy figures, weighted at the bottom, that stand up when tipped over? In Hebrew they are called קוּמָה תַּנְחוּמָא (*kumah tanhuma*), "Rise and be consoled."

There is but a short distance from rising to rising up, a distance covered in Hebrew by the reflexive form of the verb לְהִתְקוֹמֵם (*le-hitkomem*), "to revolt." In Jewish culture, the time to revolt is when the independence of the nation, the state, or the city of holiness known as Jerusalem is at stake.

Having successfully defended the קוֹמְמִיּוּת (*kommemiyut*) of these, one can proudly consider oneself as having קָם לִתְחִיָּה (*kam lit'hiyah*), been "resurrected and redeemed."

78

קרא

KOF, RESH, ALEF

CALL IT AS YOU READ IT

A Jewish response to modern times. The next time you get a voice-mail answer to your telephone call, tell the person behind the machine, "See Isaiah, chapter fifty verse two and call me back." Since the verse contains the following question, מַדּוּעַ...קָרָאתִי וְאֵין עוֹנֶה (*maddua ... karati ve-ein oneh*), "Why ... when I called, was there no one to answer?", the tactic is sure to generate a bemused reply.

The root קרא (KOF, RESH, ALEF), "to call," has generated several meanings that are fundamental to Judaism. One of them is biblical naming. A popular formula to explain the name of a person, place, or holiday in Scripture is ... עַל כֵּן קָרָא שְׁמוֹ (*al ken kara shemo ...*), "Thus was his [its] name called ..."

The Hebrew name of the Book of Leviticus derives from its first word, וַיִּקְרָא (*va-yikra*), "He called." Rashi comments that when God calls to Moses using this verb it is out of love. Other cultures have universalized several verses using our root, from Isaiah's קוֹל קוֹרֵא בַּמִּדְבָּר (*kol kore ba-midbar*), "A voice cries out in the wilderness," to King David's expression of grief, מִן הַמֵּצַר קָרָאתִי (*min ha-metsar karati*), "Out of distress I called [the Lord]," and then to the Jubilee declaration in Leviticus וּקְרָאתֶם דְּרוֹר בָּאָרֶץ (*u-keratem deror ba-arets*), "Proclaim liberty throughout the land."

The Rabbis added new meanings to the root that had reverberations beyond normative Judaism. They called the Bible מִקְרָא (*mikra*), "that which is read." When they needed a proof text, they would ask מַאי קְרָא (*mai kera*), "What is the verse [that proves this assertion]?" Originally a קָרָא (*kara*) was a "biblical scholar." In later rabbinical literature the word קָרָאִים (*kara'im*) was applied to the sect that accepted only מִקְרָא (*mikra*) and rejected rabbinic teachings, the "Karaites." An offshoot of Judaism that believed in reading was Islam; its primary text is the קוּרְאַן (*kur'an*), "that which is read."

In the synagogue today, the reading out loud of the Torah is called קְרִיאַת הַתּוֹרָה (keriyat ha-torah). One of the most profoundly moving expressions of religious love is found in the first words of the Friday-night hymn composed by the mystics of Safed, לְכָה דוֹדִי לִקְרַאת כַּלָּה (lekhah dodi likrat kallah), "Go, my beloved, to greet the [Sabbath] bride." In the Friday-night service as well, you will find a perfect example of the way the Rabbis played with biblical words for didactic effect. A word might be written one way but should be read another, for example, אַל תִּקְרִי בָּנַיִךְ אֶלָּא בּוֹנַיִךְ (al tikrei banaiyikh ella bonaiyikh), "Do not read 'your children,' but 'your builders.'"

Speaking of the didactic mode, one of the most important skills taught in Israeli schools, in addition to קְרֹא וּכְתֹב (kero u-khetov), "reading and writing," is הֲבָנַת הַנִּקְרָא (havanat ha-nikra), literally, "understanding what is written," idiomatically, "reading for comprehension."

This is a skill required not only by קַרְיָנִים (karyanim), radio "announcers," but also henceforth by telephone callers.

79

קרב

KOF, RESH, VET

NEARBRINGING

It's interesting, isn't it, how language influences the very way we accomplish our goals. Take the English word "outreach," for example, and compare it to its Hebrew equivalent, קֵרוּב (*keruv*), "nearbringing." The distinction between the two concepts may even constitute a difference.

The root of the word, קרב (KOF, RESH, VET), means "to approach," "come near," "befriend." Already in the Torah the root takes on meanings that seem either its exaggeration or its opposite. We deduce that King Avimelekh — to whom Abraham had strategically ceded his wife, Sarah — did not have sexual relations with her from the verse that tells us that the king לֹא קָרַב אֵלֶיהָ (*lo karav elehah*), literally, "did not approach her." This use of the verb קָרַב (*karav*) as a euphemism for "sexual intercourse" appears frequently in both biblical and rabbinic literature. Indeed, there is even a term קָרְבָה (*korvah*) for a woman who permits herself to be approached for sexual favors. As tempting as it might be, this word is not to be confused with the Yiddish word for prostitute, *kurveh*. The honor for originating that term belongs, we are told, to the Slavic languages and even to the Romance group, as a cognate perhaps of the English word "curve," designating someone who has veered from the straight and narrow.

Far more frequently in the Bible we see the verb לְהַקְרִיב (*le-hakriv*), "to sacrifice," and the noun קָרְבָּן (*korban*), "sacrifice." Since the root meaning of the English word "sacrifice" is "to make holy," the question arises: Why did the ancient Hebrews prefer to say that they were bringing an animal near to God rather than making it holy? The question is further complicated by a biblical word for battle, קְרָב (*kerav*), which signified originally a "drawing near" to the enemy.

A more profound sense of the word comes from a thundering command that appears seven times in the Bible, וּבִעַרְתָּ הָרָע מִקִּרְבֶּךָ

(*u-viarta ha-ra mi-kirbekha*), "You shall eradicate evil from your midst." It's easy to see how קֶרֶב (*kerev*), "midst," is related to קֶרֶב (*kerev*), "intestines." Both imply depth. Poetically mixing the two, the way you say in modern Hebrew "Thanks from the bottom of my heart" is תּוֹדָה מִקֶּרֶב לֵב (*toda mi-kerev lev*).

A *mazal tov* in Israel often elicits the Hebrew response בְּקָרוֹב אֶצְלְךָ (*be-karov etslekha*), the only good English translation for which – however inaccurate – is the Yinglish *Imyirtzehashem by you*; in English, "May God grant the same to you." If you're lucky enough to have קְרוֹבִים (*kerovim*), "relatives," in Israel, ask them to take you to the movies and make sure to get there in time for the בְּקָרוֹב (*be-karov*), a slangy noun made out of the adverb for "soon" and applied to the soon-to-be-screened "coming attraction."

When you sincerely wish to see someone again in the near future, you may want to take leave by saying לְהִתְרָאוֹת בְּקָרוֹב (*le-hitra'ot be-karov*), "See you soon."

80

קרן

KOF, RESH, NUN

LIGHTS, FUNDING, ACTION

Was Michelangelo misreading the Hebrew root קרן (KOF, RESH, NUN) when he put horns on his famous statue of Moses, our lawgiver? Perhaps he was merely following the lead of Rashi, who in his commentary on the verse קָרַן עוֹר פָּנָיו (*karan or panav*), "The skin of his [Moses'] face sent forth beams" (Exodus 34), remarks that both "beam" and "horn" stem from the same root. As Rashi explains, "Light radiates from a point and projects like a horn."

Indeed, קֶרֶן (*keren*) has so many uses in Hebrew that it would be wise, in considering the word, to think twice before assigning to it a specific meaning. In the Bible for example, קֶרֶן (*keren*) is a noun used to designate more than just a horn or a ray of light. It is also used metaphorically to indicate a person's strength and glory, as in the expression קַרְנֵי הוֹד (*karnei hod*), "horns of glory." In the Bible, as indeed in modern Hebrew, the word קֶרֶן (*keren*) can also be a girl's name. The name of Job's third daughter is קֶרֶן הַפּוּךְ (*keren hapukh*), which means either a "gleaming jewel" or a "horn filled with eye makeup." Go figure.

A קֶרֶן (*keren*), "horn," is sometimes a musical instrument, such as a *shofar*, sometimes a container, like the one in which, in olden days, travelers would store their liquid refreshment, and, in other contexts, the place where a prophet might store oil for anointing a king.

Another meaning of קֶרֶן (*keren*) relates to its pointedness. The Hebrew word קַרְנַף (*karnaf*), "rhinoceros," is a combination of the nouns קֶרֶן (*keren*), "horn," and אַף (*af*), "nose." Does the Talmud get its expression קַרְנוּנָא (*karnuna*) "stupid person," from this bovine aspect or does it come from the expression for one who hangs out on street corners, a יוֹשֵׁב קְרָנוֹת (*yoshev keranot*), an "idler"? It's likely that popular Hebrew gets its name for a cuckold, a בַּעַל קַרְנַיִם (*ba'al karnayim*), from the Romance languages, for example, the Italian *cornuto*.

Probably the most sublime use of the word in modern Israel re-

---

lates to a totally different meaning of the word, having to do with money, or capital. The קֶרֶן קַיֶּמֶת לְיִשְׂרָאֵל (keren kayemet le-yisrael), the Jewish National Fund, has made this use of the word קֶרֶן (keren) famous. There are all sorts of endowment funds and foundations in Israel, all of them collectively known as קְרָנוֹת (keranot).

The root comes full circle when we relate Michelangelo's concrete sculpture to the cinema, the evanescent modern art that is totally dependent on light. A הַקְרָנָה (hakranah) is a "film screening" that you might attend at Jerusalem's Cinémathèque, another of the glories of Israeli culture.

81

רגל

RESH, GIMMEL, LAMED

BEST FOOT FORWARD

We all know the story, recounted in the Talmud, of the Gentile who challenges the sage Hillel to teach him the entire Torah while standing עַל רֶגֶל אַחַת (al regel ahat), "on one foot." But do we realize how wittily Hillel responds, rising to the challenge by playing on the word רֶגֶל (regel), "foot"? Since רֶגֶל (regel) is a cognate of words having to do with regulations, Hillel gives the Gentile not the whole Torah but one fundamental rule, a *regula* in Latin.

The plural of רֶגֶל (regel) is found in the Torah in the expression שָׁלֹשׁ רְגָלִים (shalosh regalim), which would usually mean "three feet." Instead, רְגָלִים (regalim) here means "times," as in "Three times a year shall you celebrate."

According to one interpretation, since in those days people went to Jerusalem on foot, the three times of celebrating came to mean the three on-foot pilgrimage festivals of Pessah, Shavuot, and Sukkot. A Hebrew and English Lexicon of the Old Testament edited by Francis Brown with the cooperation of S. R. Driver and Charles A. Briggs (Oxford: Clarendon Press, 1952), has a slightly more prosaic explanation: The two biblical synonyms for "time" (as in once, twice, three times), רֶגֶל (regel) and פַּעַם (pa'am), both originally meant "footstep." This would explain why Bilaam, the prophet sent in vain by Balak to curse the Israelites, beats his donkey שָׁלֹשׁ רְגָלִים (shalosh regalim), "three times," without reference to pilgrimage festivals, before he understands God's message that he should utter blessings.

Words can teach us other things about daily life in ancient cultures. To learn that in the time of Israel's kings, laundry was done by stomping on wet clothes with one's feet, we need only look at עֵין רוֹגֵל (ein rogel), "the well of the foot treaders," a place just south of the Old City of Jerusalem.

A third meaning of our root has to do with רִגּוּל (riggul), "spying."

The name given to the twelve scouts sent by Moses to spy out the Land is מְרַגְּלִים (*meraglim*), "spies." There are some who suggest that the root רגל (RESH, GIMMEL, LAMED) is related to רכל (RESH, KHAF, LAMED), "to slander." Perhaps that's why the ten spies who spoke negatively of the Land were punished: they were slanderers. This conjecture may yet have a leg to stand on, or as they say in Hebrew, יֵשׁ רַגְלַיִם לַדָּבָר (*yesh raglayim la-davar*), "It is conceivable."

In modern Hebrew, something רָגִיל is "usual." As usual, כָּרָגִיל (*ka-ragil*), almost every *Shabbat* in the synagogue of Hovevei Zion Street in Jerusalem, an announcement is made that לְרֶגֶל הוּלֶדֶת יֶלֶד (*le-regel huledet yeled*), "in honor of the birth of a child," a *kiddush* will be served.

When a business in Israel is built on a shaky foundation, one says that it is built עַל רַגְלֵי תַּרְנְגֹלֶת (*al raglei tarnegolet*), "on chicken legs." When a business fails, we say פָּשַׁט אֶת הָרֶגֶל (*pashat et ha-regel*), "It over-extended its leg" (and therefore fell down).

Anybody who seriously wishes to perfect his or her Hebrew will acquire a תַּרְגִּילוֹן (*targilon*), "workbook," and regularly do all the תַּרְגִּילִים (*targilim*), "exercises." The work may seem tedious at first, but אַתֶּם תִּתְרַגְּלוּ לָזֶה (*atem titraglu la-zeh*), "you'll get used to it."

After all, nobody expects to learn Hebrew עַל רֶגֶל אַחַת (*al regel ahat*).

82

רחם

RESH, HET, MEM

THE QUALITY OF MERCY

There are many expressions used to describe the Jews – among them "The Chosen People," "The People of the Book," and most recently in vogue, thanks to a book by that name, "A Certain People." One of the national descriptors that Jews themselves have historically had a particular fondness for is the expression רַחֲמָנִים בְּנֵי רַחֲמָנִים (*rahamanim benei rahamanim*), "a merciful people, offspring of merciful people." The root רחם (RESH, HET, MEM), therefore, occupies a special place in the culture of the Jews.

The verb, in its simple form רָחַם (*raham*), means quite simply "He loved," and that's the way it is often used in biblical and rabbinic literature, although in modern Hebrew that sense has fallen into disuse. In the *pi'el* form, רִחֵם (*rihem*), the verb has the meaning most often attached to it today, "He had mercy." Both verbs are related to the noun רֶחֶם (*rehem*), "womb," and it takes no stretch of the imagination whatsoever to see maternal instincts at the base of the root. One of the descriptors of God is הָרַחֲמָן (*ha-rahaman*), "Merciful One," denoting the Deity's compassionate side, as distinct from His "just" side.

Nouns using this root are found most often in Hebrew either in the feminine form רַחֲמָנוּת (*rahamanut*) – from which we get the Yiddish *rakhmones* – or in the plural רַחֲמִים (*rahamim*), "pity." Two proper names derived from our root, popular among oriental Jews in Israel, are רַחֲמִים (*rahamin*), for boys, and רְחָמָה (*ruhamah*), for girls.

It is interesting that a certain vulturelike bird is called in Hebrew רָחָם (*raham*), either because it is seen in Israel at the time that much-needed rains begin to fall or because – although a bird of prey and therefore unkosher – it is supposed to care inordinately for its young.

There are many fascinating expressions in Aramaic that make use of the root רחם (RESH, HET, MEM). A halakhic principle holds that אָנוּס רַחֲמָנָא פְּטַרֵהּ (*anus rahamana petareh*), "If one should commit a sin against his will, the Merciful One acquits him." And then there is the expression that everyone uses on hearing of a terrible occurrence, רַחֲמָנָא לִצְלָן (*rahamana litslan*), "May the Merciful One save us [from that]." So frequently is this last expression used that you'll often see it abbreviated ר"ל (RESH, LAMED).

Fortunately for us, as they say, "The quality of mercy is not strained," even when efforts to understand the roots of Hebrew words may be strained beyond credulity.

83

רחץ

RESH, HET, TSADI

WASHERS AND PURIFIERS

You can tell a good deal about the Jewish people from the activities they engage in with great frequency. An especially revealing activity – found in a great variety of ritual practice – is washing.

There are several Hebrew roots for washing, as we can see from the expressions for ritual hand washing, נְטִילַת יָדַיִם (*netilat yadayim*), and bodily immersion, טְבִילָה (*tevilah*). But the richest root is רחץ (RESH, HET, TSADI), from which we get the nouns רַחַץ (*rahats*), רַחְצָה (*rahtsah*), רְחִיצָה (*rehitsah*), and רַחְצָה (*rohtsah*), all of which mean "washing" or "bathing."

It might be said that bathing is at the origin of the Exodus from Egypt. After all, are we not told that the baby Moses' life was saved when Pharaoh's daughter went down לִרְחֹץ עַל הַיְאֹר (*lirhots al ha-e'or*), "to bathe at the Nile," and there found the infant in a basket?

The root occurs twice in the order of the Passover Seder. The second ritual after the *kiddush* is called וּרְחַץ (*u-rehats*), calling for an ablution before the eating of greens; the sixth rite is called רַחְצָה (*rahtsah*) and refers to the washing of the hands between the telling of the traditional Passover story and the eating of the *matsah*.

In the Bible washing is associated with both hospitality and eroticism. The patriarch Abraham welcomes his guests by rushing out to greet them and saying יֻקַּח נָא מְעַט מַיִם וְרַחֲצוּ רַגְלֵיכֶם (*yukakh na me'at mayim ve-rahatsu ragleikhem*), "Let some water be taken and wash your feet." The lover in the Song of Songs compares the teeth of his beloved to a flock of white ewes שֶׁעָלוּ מִן הָרַחְצָה (*she-alu min ha-rahatsah*), "coming up from the bath." And of course, King David's first contact with Bathsheba, the mother of the man who would write the Song of Songs, is the vision of a woman רֹחֶצֶת מֵעַל הַגָּג (*rohetset me-al ha-gag*), "bathing on the roof."

In modern Hebrew, the root is found in the expression בֵּית מֶרְחָץ

(*beit merhats*), "public bath," in the name for a private washroom in one's home, חֲדַר רַחְצָה (*hadar rahtsah*), in the reflexive verb לְהִתְרַחֵץ (*le-hitrahets*), "to get washed," and in the noun for that obsessive person who washes frequently, רַחְצָן (*rahtsan*).

Of course, if we looked purely at Jewish ritual practice, we would conclude that the Jews as a people are not merely obsessively frequent washers but rather that they are aiming for a spiritually higher level, that of purifiers.

84
רשם
RESH, SHIN, MEM
FIRST IMPRESSIONS

Everybody wants to make a good first impression, to be sure. In Israel, one way to make a רֹשֶׁם טוֹב (*roshem tov*), a "good impression," is to use the Hebrew language with dexterity. Show, for example, how many words you can derive from the root רשם (RESH, SHIN, MEM) and you will impress many.

The root occurs in the *Tanakh* only in the Book of Daniel, where it is used in the form of רָשׁוּם (*rashum*), "inscribed." One need only think of the provebial use of the Book of Daniel's "handwriting on the wall" to realize how language can move from a concrete activity, like writing, to its abstract analog, impressing. In the Talmud, people who are inclined to interpret the law metaphorically are called דוֹרְשֵׁי רְשׁוּמוֹת (*dorshei rishumot*), "expounders of impressions."

The concrete uses of the root in modern-day Israel are many. When you wish to take an adult-education course at the Buber Institute of the Hebrew University, for example, you go during the הַרְשָׁמָה (*harshamah*), "registration period," לְהֵרָשֵׁם (*le-hirashem*), "to register." You will find out when that is if you are on their רְשִׁימַת הַנִּמְעָנִים (*reshimat ha-nimanim*), "mailing list."

A list you will try to avoid is the metaphorical רְשִׁימָה שְׁחוֹרָה (*reshimah shehorah*), "blacklist." Curiously, Hebrew slang has concocted, where English has not, the idea of a "white list," רְשִׁימָה לְבָנָה (*reshimah levanah*), where you will find "inscribed" what Hebrew calls אַנְשֵׁי שְׁלוֹמֵינוּ (*anshei shelomeinu*), one's "cronies." A good example of what the Mediterranean climate has done to the Hebrew language can be seen from the idiom לִרְשֹׁם עַל הַקֶּרַח (*lirshom al ha-kerah*), literally "to inscribe on ice," in figurative English, "to write on the wind."

To write something down is to make it official. That is the logical conclusion to draw from the existence of the adjective רִשְׁמִי (*rishmi*), "official." (On the street you will also frequently hear its Arabic cognate *rasmi*.) The name of the Israel government's official gazette is רְשׁוּמוֹת (*reshumot*). There you might find a תַּרְשִׁים (*tarshim*), a "diagram" or "sketch," of a housing plan for new immigrants, one that permits you לְהִתְרַשֵּׁם (*le-hitrashem*), "to be impressed" by the government's work.

After all, politicians, above all, want to make a רֹשֶׁם טוֹב (*roshem tov*).

85

שאל

SHIN, ALEF, LAMED

WHO ASKED YOU?

In Judaism what is more important, the question or the answer? Is it not curious that the English word to describe the vast body of Jewish writing called Responsa should focus only on the answer, while the Hebrew expression for it, שְׁאֵלוֹת וּתְשׁוּבוֹת (she'elot u-teshuvot), "questions and answers," should give equal emphasis to both? And who would have guessed that one of the first books written after the close of the Talmud would be called שְׁאֵלְתּוֹת (she'iltot), "questions"?

Is it not natural that during the first days of spring, when nature itself takes on a certain indeterminacy, Jewish life should revolve around questions? How else are we going to explain the central place in the Passover *haggadah* of the אַרְבַּע קוּשְׁיוֹת (arba kushiyot), the "four questions," in Yiddish *di fir kashes?* And what about the popular question-song chanted toward the end of the Seder, אֶחָד מִי יוֹדֵעַ (ehad mi yo-de'a), "Who knows one?"

What is at the root of all this questioning, if not the *shoresh* שאל (SHIN, ALEF, LAMED), "to ask"? And the source? How about the verse in Exodus, וְהָיָה כִּי יִשְׁאָלְךָ בִנְךָ מָחָר לֵאמֹר מַה זֹּאת (ve-hayah ki yesh'alkha binkha mahar leimor mah zot), "When on the morrow your son shall ask: 'What is this?'"

Where in the *Tanakh* does the verb שָׁאַל (sha'al) not take a סִימַן שְׁאֵלָה (siman she'elah), "question mark"? On leaving Egypt, how did the Israelites get reimbursement for their years of slave labor, except by asking for it from the Egyptians with our *shoresh*, וַיְּשָׁאֲלוּם (va-yash'ilum)? And what do you think King David's one request from God was – אַחַת שָׁאַלְתִּי מֵאֵת ה' (ahat sha'alti me-et ha-shem) – if not to dwell in God's house?

Why is the prophet Samuel called Samuel? Does not his mother Hannah explain, כִּי מֵה' שְׁאִלְתִּיו (ki me-ha-shem she'iltiv), "for I requested him of God"? But in that case, shouldn't his name have been not שְׁמוּאֵל (shemuel), Samuel, but שָׁאוּל (sha'ul), Saul? It's an enigma, isn't it?

Did you know that a שׁוֹאֵל (sho'el) in Hebrew is not only a questioner but a borrower and that, for example, a מִלָּה שְׁאוּלָה (millah she'ulah) is a word one language borrows from another? How do we get from asking to borrowing? Is it not perhaps wisest to answer this question not with another question – as Jews are wont to do – but with a declaration on the order of אַל תִּשְׁאַל (al tish'al), don't ask? Or are you perhaps democratically inclined and prefer to call for a מִשְׁאָל (mish'al), "referendum," on it, or at least be asked to fill out a שְׁאֵלוֹן (she'elon), a "questionnaire"?

Did you get it?

86

שכן

SHIN, KHAF, NUN

FLOCKING TOGETHER

It is said that the wisdom of nations is contained in their proverbs, pithy sayings that express – from deep inside the community – the community's values. Take, for example, the English expression "Birds of a feather flock together." While the Hebrew version, כָּל עוֹף לְמִינוֹ יִשְׁכּוֹן (*kol of le-mino yishkon*), "Each bird dwells with its own species," expresses an essentially equivalent sentiment, there is a discernible qualitative difference in the use of the Hebrew verb לִשְׁכֹּן (*lishkon*), "to dwell," which implies that the Jewish bird strives to make a permanent community.

The three letters שכן (SHIN, KHAF, NUN) are at the root of a number of words that relate the history and express the values of the Jewish people. In the biblical story of Bilaam, a foreign prophet sent to curse the Israelites, we are told that because מִשְׁכְּנוֹתֶיךָ יִשְׂרָאֵל (*mishkenote-kha yisrael*), "thy dwellings, Israel," are "good," Bilaam can only utter the admittedly strange blessing that Israel shall be an עָם לְבָדָד יִשְׁכֹּן (*am levadad yishkon*), "a nation that dwells apart."

Dwelling apart does not necessarily mean living alone, because, for the Jews, there is the שְׁכִינָה (*shekhinah*), "Divine Presence," dwelling among them.

And then there is the מִשְׁכָּן (*mishkan*), the "Tabernacle," erected by the Israelites in the desert after their liberation from Egypt. The word מִשְׁכָּן (*mishkan*) is playfully related by the Rabbis to the word מַשְׁכּוֹן (*mashkon*), "pledge," that is, a piece of property held as a guaranty for a debt. The Rabbis said that when the Israelites deserved a punishment, the מִשְׁכָּן (*mishkan*) was seized by God and became a מַשְׁכּוֹן (*mashkon*), "pledge," until it would be redeemed by an act of *teshuvah* (repentance) on the part of Israel.

Nowadays, the way Israelis guarantee a debt is to pledge their apartment, acquiring in the process a מַשְׁכַּנְתָּה (*mashkantah*), "mortgage."

A community of like-minded people in Israel might live together in a שִׁכּוּן (*shikkun*), "housing project," or artists and writers might flock to Jerusalem's prestigious מִשְׁכְּנוֹת שַׁאֲנַנִים (*mishkenot sha'ananim*), "habitations of tranquillity." Community can be a two-edged sword, however, as evidenced by the Jewish proverb אוֹי לָרָשָׁע אוֹי לִשְׁכֵנוֹ (*oy la-rasha oy lishkheno*), "Woe to the evildoer and woe to his neighbor."

But then again, there is Project Renewal — based on faith in the Jewish version of "birds of a feather." Project Renewal was able to take the depressed neighborhood of Tel Aviv called שְׁכוּנַת הַתִּקְוָה (*shekhunat ha-tikvah*) and turn it from a slum into a place where, if the *Shekhinah* does not yet dwell there comfortably, at least תִּקְוָה (*tikvah*), "hope," does.

87

שמן

SHIN, MEM, NUN

OIL DEFINERY

What do Ashkenazic potato *latkes* have in common with Sephardic סוּפְגָנִיּוֹת (*sufganiyot*), "doughnuts"? They are both foods eaten traditionally at Hanukkah. The שֶׁמֶן (*shemen*), "oil," they are fried in commemorates the miracle that took place when a single measure of oil found in the desecrated Temple supplied light for eight days.

When an Israeli physician was asked the same question about pancakes and doughnuts, his reply was predictably clinical: both *latkes* and *sufganiyot* are מַשְׁמִינִים (*mashminim*, plural; the singular is מַשְׁמִין [*mashmin*], "fattening," and should be eaten in moderation).

And yet, the adjective שָׁמֵן (*shamen*), "fat," is not totally pejorative. In fact, not all Hebrew speakers adhere to the American adage coined by Madison Avenue, "you can't be too rich or too thin." In Hebrew, it is often the case that to be fat is also to be rich. Take, for example, the expression בּוֹר שֶׁמָן (*bor shumman*); it is not only a literal "tub of lard," it is also figuratively a "profitable business."

To be or to become שָׁמֵן (*shamen*), "fat," is not necessarily a comment on one's state of health. When the Torah wishes to emphasize that the Israelites defeated in battle the best of the Moabite soldiers, it describes the latter as כָּל שָׁמֵן וְכָל אִישׁ חָיִל (*kol shamen ve-khol ish hayyil*), "every lusty and valiant man."

Rabbinic Hebrew has a lovely expression for the making of compromises. When the path between two sides in a conflict has patches of roughness, the Rabbis suggest that מַשְׁמִינִים בֵּינֵיהֶם (*mashminim beineihem*), "we add a layer of grease." This serves to smooth out the road between them so that they can make a compromise.

In modern Hebrew, a pudgy fellow is called a שְׁמַנְמַן (*shemanman*) and *latkes* are eaten with שַׁמֶּנֶת (*shammenet*), "sour cream."

Using the sweet sense of this word figuratively, General Mordecai Gur, in June 1967, praised the soldiers wounded during the Six Day

---

War, characterizing them מֵהַשַּׁמֶּנֶת שֶׁבַּחֲטִיבָה (*me-ha-shammenet she-ba-hati-vah*), "from the cream of the brigade."

There are several other idiomatic expressions that use the root שמן (SHIN, MEM, NUN) to denote excellence. A particularly colorful one is הוא מְדַבֵּר שֶׁמֶן זַיִת זַךְ (*hu medabber shemen zayit zakh*), "He speaks pure olive oil"; that is, his words are as precious as the oil in the Hanukkah *menorah*.

According to the Rabbis, there is something more precious than even the best of oils, a precious commodity indeed. As they put it in an aphorism, טוֹב שֵׁם מִשֶּׁמֶן טוֹב (*tov shem mi-shemen tov*), "A good name, that is, reputation, is better than a good oil."

When the oil illuminates a whole people's good name, then you have Hanukkah.

88

שמע

SHIN, MEM, AYIN

THE ART OF THE SCHMOOZE

If there is one Hebrew word that most Jews have at least heard, it is the word שְׁמַע (shema), "Hear." That is the first word heard when a Jew begins to recite שְׁמַע יִשְׂרָאֵל (shema yisrael), the Jewish declaration of belief in one God: "Hear O Israel, the Lord our God, the Lord is One."

The root שמע (SHIN, MEM, AYIN) is heard in a host of other contexts as well. Sh'ma, for example, is the name of an eight-page American periodical, published by the Center for Leadership and Learning (CLAL), that permits the airing of varied opinions on Jewish life.

To some people, it might seem strange that the first word of the Jewish credo is "hear" rather than "say," especially since the best way to affirm one's belief is to proclaim it. Perhaps the reason for the choice of our root is that it means not only "to hear" but also "to understand."

The root also contains the sense of "to obey." When a teacher has obedient, well-behaved students in a class, she or he has מִשְׁמַעַת (mishma'at), "discipline." The root therefore has more than one מַשְׁמָעוּת (mashma'ut), "meaning," and while this root may indeed be רַב מַשְׁמָעִי (rav mashma'i), the bearer of "many meanings," the credo expressed by the Shema can only be said to be חַד מַשְׁמָעִי (had mashma'i), "unambiguous."

In the Bible we learn that Jacob's second son was named שִׁמְעוֹן (shim'on), "Simon," because, as his mother Leah said, שָׁמַע ה' כִּי שְׂנוּאָה אָנֹכִי (shama ha-shem ki senu'ah anokhi), "God has heard that I am hated." In Psalms we are asked to praise God with צִלְצְלֵי שָׁמַע (tsiltselei shama), "resounding cymbals." When the Rabbis of the Talmud wanted to know the meaning of a certain episode, they would ask, in Aramaic, מַאי קָא מַשְׁמַע לָן (mai ka mashma lan), "What does this teach us?" When the meaning of a word was evident, they would say פְּשׁוּטוֹ כְּמַשְׁמָעוֹ (peshuto ke-mashma'o), "It means what it says."

Since Israeli Hebrew is highly allusive to the Jewish textual tradition, these expressions have found their way into daily modern Hebrew conversation as well. A sharply beautiful Hebrew way of pointing out that the person you are talking to is contradicting himself is to say יִשְׁמְעוּ אָזְנֶיךָ מַה שֶּׁפִּיךָ מְדַבֵּר (*yishme'u oznekha mah she-pikha medabber*), "Let your ears hear what your mouth is saying."

It is not strange that the noun for hearing שְׁמִיעָה (*shemiyah*), and the noun for rumor שְׁמוּעָה (*shemu'ah*), should derive from the root שמע (SHIN, MEM, AYIN). But did you ever realize that the Yiddish-English verb "to schmooze" is built on the Ashkenazic pronunciation of the plural form of the word שְׁמוּעָה (*shemu'ah*)? To exchange gossip or *shemu'os* is, by extension, to schmooze. A cartoon in the *New Yorker Magazine* has one character assert to his business associate, "The Information Superhighway will never replace the art of the schmooze."

Schmoozing is certainly what you'll want to do the next time someone asks you מַה נִּשְׁמָע (*mah nishma*), "What's new?"

89

שמש

SHIN, MEM, SHIN

INSTRUMENTALITY

In Hebrew, when you talk about the sources of a word, you're not just talking about etymology; as often as not, you're also talking about theology. Take the case of the humble שַׁמָּשׁ (shammash), the auxiliary candle found on the traditional Hanukkah *menorah*.

The laws of Hanukkah state that we are not permitted to use the Hanukkah candle for either light or fire: אֵין לָנוּ רְשׁוּת לְהִשְׁתַּמֵּשׁ בָּהֶם (ein lanu reshut le-hishtamesh bahem), with the emphasis on לְהִשְׁתַּמֵּשׁ (le-hish-tamesh), "to use." Consequently, we take the root of the verb לְהִשְׁתַּמֵּשׁ (le-hishtamesh), שמש (SHIN, MEM, SHIN), and create a candle, the (sham-mash), that we use to kindle the others. The שַׁמָּשׁ (shammash) has no intrinsic value; it is an instrument that takes its importance from its very instrumentality, like a servant.

Followers of Hebrew etymology will not fail to note the similarities between שַׁמָּשׁ (shammash), "servant," and שֶׁמֶשׁ (shemesh), "sun." Is there a connection? We do know that in the ancient Near East, one of the forms of idolatry was heliolatry, sun worship, and that various sun goddesses had names similar to our word for sun. In pagan culture, the sun had value; it was god. Did not Judaism take this sun-god and transform it into the servant of the one God, transforming the שֶׁמֶשׁ (shemesh) of the pagans into a שַׁמָּשׁ (shammash), a servant of God?

Instrumentality is also the essence of the synagogue sexton, or שַׁמָּשׁ (shammash); he is known to most of us in his Yiddish pronunciation, *shammes*. This pronunciation has led to a well-worn character found in mystery novels, the "shamus," the detective who owes his slang name to our root.

Euphemism is particularly important in rabbinic literature, and the שמש (SHIN, MEM, SHIN) root also has its euphemistic value. In modern Hebrew a בֵּית שִׁמּוּשׁ (beit shimmush), "house of usefulness," is the way one characterizes a bathroom. The Talmud calls the male genera-

---

tive organ a שַׁמָּשׁ (*shammash*), an "instrument" of procreation; the performance of one's marital duty is characterized תַּשְׁמִישׁ הַמִּטָּה (*tashmish ha-mittah*), "the use of the bed." This last is not to be confused with articles used in the performance of purely religious rituals, like the Hanukkah *menorah*, which are called תַּשְׁמִישֵׁי קְדוּשָׁה (*tashmishei kedushah*), "instruments of holiness."

Is this etymology or theology? It may be speculative, but it is one way of using an instrument to talk about Hebrew.

90
שער

SHIN, AYIN, RESH
RATES AND GATES

One of the first pieces of information you're likely to pick up about Israel as you pass through Ben Gurion Airport is whether the שַׁעַר הַחֲלִיפִין (sha'ar ha-halifin), the "rate of exchange," has remained relatively stable. While you might want to consult your local economist to explain how the rates are set, your הַשְׁעָרָה (hash'arah), "conjecture," might be just as good as anyone's. Since conjecture is at the root of books about Hebrew words, it is appropriate that we look at the Hebrew root שער (SHIN, AYIN, RESH).

The noun שַׁעַר (sha'ar) was originally used to denote a broad opening in the city wall. According to the Torah, a biblical quotation was to be hung not only on the *mezuzot* of the doors of one's house but also בִּשְׁעָרֶיךָ (bish'arekha), "on thy gates." A visitor to the Old City of Jerusalem will often pass through שַׁעַר יָפוֹ (sha'ar yafo), Jaffa Gate. The word שַׁעַר (sha'ar) is also used symbolically as an opening into the religious realm, as in שַׁעֲרֵי תְּפִלָּה (sha'arei tefillah), "gates of prayer," an expression that is also the name for both a synagogue and a prayer book.

In Israel, the word שַׁעַר (sha'ar) can be found most often on the lips of sports fans, specifically among the vast number of Israelis addicted to soccer. For them, a שַׁעַר (sha'ar) is a "goal," a שַׁעַר נִצָּחוֹן (sha'ar nitsahon) is the score your star forward makes to turn a 2–2 tie into a 3–2 victory, and a שַׁעַר כָּבוֹד (sha'ar kavod) is that goal that preserves your team's honor in a 7–1 defeat, thus avoiding a shutout. The goalkeeper in soccer is called a שׁוֹעֵר (sho'er), a word reserved in everyday speech for your building's porter.

To get from soccer back to the idea of measurement, a bit of conjecture is in order. The שַׁעַר (sha'ar) is not only the city gate but also the space within the gate, often a marketplace. The שַׁעַר (sha'ar) would then be both the place where the price is set, the market, and the price itself, the "market."

The ultra-Orthodox Jerusalem neighborhood of מֵאָה שְׁעָרִים (*me'ah she'arim*) got its name not from its one hundred gates (which it does not have) but because originally there were one hundred parcels of land to be divided up. The land developers took the name from the Book of Genesis, where *me'ah she'arim* means "a hundred portions."

This lesson of Hebrew language learning is called a שִׁעוּר (*shiur*). For שִׁעוּרֵי בַּיִת (*shiurei bayit*), "homework," let's try to pick up some new Hebrew idioms during our next vacation.

A good place to start would be the change window at Ben Gurion Airport.

91

שׁפח

SHIN, FEH, HET

FAMILY TIES

Is family a fundamental Jewish value? Is a bluebird blue? The textual evidence for the centrality of מִשְׁפָּחָה (*mishpahah*), "family," in Jewish history is overwhelming. In what must be a record for concentrated frequency of a word in Scripture, מִשְׁפָּחָה (*mishpahah*) appears in a single chapter of the Book of Numbers no fewer than eighty-seven times, designating the more than sixty מִשְׁפָּחוֹת (*mishpahot*) that made up the people of Israel during their forty-year trek in the desert.

The most curious thing about the history of the word מִשְׁפָּחָה (*mishpahah*) is its not-so-evident relationship to the Hebrew word for female domestic servant, שִׁפְחָה (*shifhah*). Our foremother Sarah, fearful that she would not be able to have a family of her own, tells her husband to father a child with Sarah's servant Hagar. The child of the שִׁפְחָה (*shifhah*) would then be considered part of the מִשְׁפָּחָה (*mishpahah*), "family," of Abraham and Sarah.

To underscore the relationship between *shifhah* and *mishpahah*, we need only look at the Latin word for family, *familia*, whose first meaning is "household slaves" and which only susbsequently came to mean "household." Thus, on two etymological counts, you need not feel reluctant to tell your children to take out the garbage.

Some years ago, a joke about advertising slogans circulated in New York banking circles. In response to the slogan "You have a friend at Chase Manhattan," some wag came up with the rejoinder "But at Bank Le'eumi you have *mishpokhe*." In scientific Hebrew, the word מִשְׁפָּחָה (*mishpahah*) is a tool of classification to denote a family of plants, animals, or languages. In colloquial speech, the word retains a sense of intimacy. The Hebrew equivalent of the Yiddish word *heimish* is מִשְׁפַּחְתִּי (*mishpahti*). The noun מִשְׁפַּחְתִּיּוּת (*mishpahti'ut*) means both "intimacy" and "comfortable simplicity." A traditional term for a family celebration is זֶבַח מִשְׁפָּחָה (*zevah mishpahah*). The use of the word זֶבַח

(*zevah*), meaning "sacrifice," is a reminder that in the days of the temple, many sacrifices, especially the Paschal lamb, were eaten in the bosom of one's family.

A family man is a בַּעַל מִשְׁפָּחָה (*ba'al mishpahah*). Your family name is your שֵׁם מִשְׁפָּחָה (*shem mishpahah*). On your next trip to Israel, you might get one of those gaily decorated ceramic doorplates inscribed with your שֵׁם מִשְׁפָּחָה (*shem mishpahah*) in Hebrew — for example, מִשְׁפַּחַת לֵוִי (*mishpahat levi*) or מִשְׁפַּחַת כֹּהֵן (*mishpahat kohen*), the "Levy" or "Cohen" families. It will identify you proudly as a member of מִשְׁפַּחַת יִשְׂרָאֵל (*mishpahat yisrael*), the Family of Israel.

92

שֶׁקֶל

SHIN, KOF, LAMED

WEIGHTY MATTERS

There was a time, so it seemed, when every conversation in Israel would begin and end with פֶּצֶ'ה מֶצֶ'ה (*petsheh-metsheh*). This word borrowed from the Yiddish and meaningfully accompanied by the gesture of rubbing the thumb against the index and middle fingers, was universally understood to mean "money."

Now that the colonial לִירָה (*lirah*), "pound," has been replaced by the Jewish שֶׁקֶל (*shekel*), itself superseded by the שֶׁקֶל חָדָשׁ (*shekel hadash*), the "new (and improved) shekel," people still talk about the economy, but these days they feel they can do something about it.

The modern Israeli shekel has a fascinating background, both semantic and historical. It comes from the verb לִשְׁקֹל (*lishkol*), "to weigh." Originally, payment was made by weighing out a quantity of precious metal, whether gold or silver, or sometimes copper or iron. Eventually, coins were struck using one or the other of these metals, each having a specific weight. The silver שֶׁקֶל (*shekel*), weighing 7.2 grams, gained the greatest currency (pun absolutely intended). The Hebrew word כֶּסֶף (*kesef*), "silver," is today the generic word for "money."

The shekel was used not only in commerce but also for ritual purposes. The מַחֲצִית הַשֶּׁקֶל (*mahatsit ha-shekel*), the half-shekel, was collected from every citizen in taking the head count of the ancient Israelites. The שֶׁקֶל הַקֹּדֶשׁ (*shekel ha-kodesh*), literally, the "holy shekel," double the weight of the ordinary shekel, was part of the donation made by the heads of the Israelite tribes during the consecration of the Tabernacle. In the modern period, Zionist leaders would purchase a shekel from the World Zionist Organization as a token of their membership in the movement.

Another historical reference to the word שֶׁקֶל (*shekel*) can be found in the Jewish liturgical calendar. The *Shabbat* before the month of *Adar*, during which Purim is celebrated, is called פָּרָשַׁת שְׁקָלִים (*parashat sheka-*

---

lim) to remind us that wicked Haman was willing to pay – אֶשְׁקוֹל (*eshkol*), "I will pay," is the verb he used – for the privilege of murdering Jews.

An Aramaic idiom, שַׁקְלָא וְטַרְיָא (*shakla ve-tarya*), referring to disputes in the Talmud, is sometimes used to characterize the give-and take of political negotiations, such as those held between Israel and Egypt during the negotiations concerning the Red Sea resort of Taba. One of the four words in the famous "handwriting on the wall" expression found in the Book of Daniel is תְּקֵל (*tekel*), "weigh," teaching us nothing perhaps about the meaning of the expression but showing us clearly that there is interchangeability of consonants between Hebrew and Aramaic.

The noun מִשְׁקָל (*mishkal*), "weight," has several meanings, the most frequent being that found in obesity clinics, where one goes to learn whether one has gained or lost some. In grammar, the noun מִשְׁקָל (*mishkal*) is used to designate a verbal paradigm; thus if לִשְׁקֹל (*lishkol*) is the form that means "to weigh" physically, לְשַׁקֵּל (*le-shakkel*) is the verbal class that means "to ponder," to weigh mentally.

Whether you pay in שְׁקָלִים (*shekalim*) or דּוֹלָרִים (*dolarim*), "dollars" – both of which are translatable into colloquial English as "shekels" – a good way to spend your פֶּצֶ׳ה מֶצֶ׳ה (*petsheh-metsheh*) today is to take a vacation in any of Israel's many seaside resorts.

93

שקע

SHIN, KOF, AYIN

PLUGGED IN

How can you tell when, after the investment of much time and effort, you are finally fluent in a language? One test is infallible: when you make the same mistakes made by native speakers, you have gained a measure of mastery of the language.

If, for example, it's dark in the room and you are asked to plug in an Israeli lamp, almost invariably you will be asked to put the שֶׁקַע (*sheka*), "socket," into the תֶּקַע (*teka*), "plug." If, despite the Hebrew speaker's mistake, you know enough to put the תֶּקַע (*teka*), "plug," in the שֶׁקַע (*sheka*), "socket," you are fluent. You have learned that mistakes count only when they impede communication.

The confusion arises perhaps from the uses to which the root שקע (SHIN, KOF, AYIN) is put. Originally, the verb שָׁקַע (*shaka*) meant "to sink." The prophet Jeremiah compares Babylon's inevitable demise to the sinking of a stone: כָּכָה תִּשְׁקַע בָּבֶל וְלֹא תָקוּם (*kakhah tishka bavel ve-lo takum*), "Thus shall Babylon sink and shall not rise again" (Jeremiah 51:64). The verb also contains a sense of diminishment. When, in the Book of Numbers, the Israelites are threatened by God's fire, Moses prays for relief, and וַתִּשְׁקַע הָאֵשׁ (*va-tishka ha-esh*), "the fire abated" (11:2). These biblical uses lead us to the rabbinic expression שְׁקִיעַת הַחַמָּה (*shekiyat ha-hammah*), "the setting of the sun."

In modern Hebrew, the root is put to use to convey contemporary meanings. Of a person in the public arena who has begun to lose power, you might say שָׁקְעָה הַשְׁפָּעָתוֹ (*shak'ah hashpa'ato*), "His influence has diminished." If you enter into an old house, you may notice that הָרִצְפָּה שָׁקְעָה (*ha-ritspah shak'a*), "The floor has settled."

Jews don't save money, the joke goes; they invest. When they do, they use the root שקע (SHIN, KOF, AYIN). In Israel, הַשְׁקָעַת כְּסָפִים (*hashka'at kesafim*) is the investment of money. If you put a great deal of time and effort into a project, such as the learning of Hebrew, it will be

---

said that אַתָּה מַשְׁקִיעַ מַאֲמַצִּים גְּדוֹלִים (*attah mashkiya ma'amatsim gedolim*), "You are investing great efforts."

Some people go to Israel to practice their Hebrew as תַּיָּרִים (*tay-yarim*), "tourists." Others prefer לְהִשְׁתַּקֵּעַ (*le-hishtake'a*), "to settle," in the land and to speak the language, however imperfectly. Just by looking at the verb לְהִשְׁתַּקֵּעַ (*le-hishtake'a*), with its juxtaposed שׁ (SHIN) and תּ (TAV), one could be forgiven for confusing a שֶׁקַע (*sheka*) with a תֶּקַע (*teka*). In fact, possibly the only word using our root that does not breed this confusion is שְׁקַעֲרוּרִי (*sheka'aruri*), "concave." Something concave should at least look like a receptacle or a socket.

In all cases, however, the principle is clear: When an Israeli understands and acts correctly upon your mistake, you are both speaking fluent Hebrew.

Above all, let there be light.

94

שׁקף

SHIN, KOF, FEH

ON THE LOOKOUT

In Western culture, particularly among the well-lettered, one's outlook on life is called a *Weltanschauung*. In Hebrew, it's called הַשְׁקָפַת עוֹלָם (*hashkafat olam*), "worldview."

The three-letter root שׁקף (SHIN, KOF, FEH) has served as the basis for several nouns in modern Hebrew. The fields in which the root is found range across the spectrum of human activity, including the humanities, the arts, science, and technology.

It is even found in army life. Thus, the מַשְׁקִיף הָאוּ״ם (*mashkif ha-um*), "UN observer," who is almost certainly wearing a pair of מִשְׁקְפֵי שֶׁמֶשׁ (*mishkefei shemesh*), "sunglasses," to protect his eyes from the glaring sun, will, from time to time, take out his מִשְׁקֶפֶת (*mishkefet*), "binoculars," לְהַשְׁקִיף (*le-hashkif*), "to survey" the area.

Another modern use of the root is related not to seeing but to showing. Two physicians at a celebrated hospital located in Israel were recently overheard commenting about an announcement on the bulletin board: an American expert was coming to lecture about the results of his research, "with slides." One local physician said to the other, "That's the definition of an 'expert' – someone from another country, with שְׁקוּפִיּוֹת (*shekufiyot*), 'slides.'"

The verb form of the root has many meanings related to seeing, observing, watching, surveying, reviewing. The simplest form of the verb is found in the passive, נִשְׁקַף (*nishkaf*), "to be seen," "to be visible." In another form it also means to give a true picture, as in the expression הָרוֹמָן מְשַׁקֵף אֶת חַיֵּי הַקִּיבּוּץ (*ha-roman meshakef et hayyei ha-kibbuts*), "The novel depicts kibbutz life faithfully."

In the Torah, the verb formed from the root is used about half a dozen times alongside the word חַלּוֹן (*halon*), "window." For example, Genesis 26:8 relates that after Isaac had misinformed his host that Rebecca was his sister, וַיַּשְׁקֵף אֲבִימֶלֶךְ בְּעַד הַחַלּוֹן (*va-yashkef avimelekh be-ad ha-halon*), "Avimelekh peered out the window" and saw Isaac "sporting" with Rebecca, whom the king then took to be his guest's wife. This is probably the first case in history of involuntary voyeurism. It is also, apparently, one of the earliest records of the existence of windows.

God, in biblical discourse, does not look out of windows, but from Heaven. One of the most beautiful passages in the Bible, subsequently set to music in modern Israel, is a prayer asking God to look out from His holy dwelling place and to bless His people and the Land of Israel. The verse beginning הַשְׁקִיפָה מִמְּעוֹן קָדְשְׁךָ (*hashkifah mi-me'on kodshekha*), "Look down from Your abode of holiness," can be found in Deuteronomy 26:15. Or, you might wish to purchase the recording. It all depends on your הַשְׁקָפָה (*hashkafah*).

95
שׂמח
SIN, MEM, HET
BE HAPPY, JUST DO IT

It happened on an El Al flight, eastbound. The Jewish traveler was explaining Sukkot, the Feast of Booths, to a Christian pilgrim en route to the Holy Land.

"It's also called זְמַן שִׂמְחָתֵנוּ (*zeman simkhatenu*), the Time of our Rejoicing."

"What's so enjoyable about eating and sleeping in a flimsy booth?"

"Jews are required to be joyous, even in adversity. Especially then. It's even a commandment in the Torah: וְשָׂמַחְתָּ בְּחַגֶּיךָ (*ve-samakhta be-hagekha*), 'You shall rejoice on your holy days.' Even if you're unhappy at the moment, you must celebrate the day."

"What kind of religion could require you to be happy?"

"Well, you can tell something about a religion by looking at its vocabulary. Take the word שִׂמְחָה (*simhah*), 'happiness,' for example. During Temple times there was a ceremony that took place during Sukkot that had the word שִׂמְחָה (*simhah*) in its name, שִׂמְחַת בֵּית הַשּׁוֹאֵבָה (*simhat bet ha-sho'evah*), the 'Water-Drawing Festival.' The Mishnah, describing the ceremony, talks mostly not about water but about the lighting of very tall torches in the Temple courtyard. Since ancient times, joy in Judaism has been associated with light.

"A poetic rabbinic term for a blind man is the Aramaic expression סַגִי נָהוֹר (*sagi nahor*), literally, 'There's plenty of light.' The Rabbis had a certain fastidiousness about language. Whenever they wished to avoid speaking in an offensive way, they would use what they termed לְשׁוֹן סַגִי נָהוֹר (*leshon sagi nahor*), 'the language of light,' with which they would replace 'the language of darkness.' Their way of dealing with the semantic problem of naming the talmudic tractate dealing with the laws of mourning was to call it שְׂמָחוֹת (*semahot*), the plural of the word שִׂמְחָה (*simhah*), which is of course the opposite of 'bereavement.'

"The Jews have a tradition of going מִיָּגוֹן לְשִׂמְחָה (*mi-yagon le-simhah*), 'from sorrow to joy.' Today in Israel or America a שִׂמְחָה (*sim-hah*) is any joyous occasion, a wedding or a *bar mitsvah*, what in America we call an 'affair.' The hosts are called בַּעֲלֵי שִׂמְחָה (*ba'alei simhah*). When a daughter is born, we have a new ceremony called a שִׂמְחַת בַּת (*simhat bat*) to parallel the *shalom zakhor* welcoming a baby boy.

"Of course, a living language twists its idioms every which way, often to achieve irony. Upon learning that he has a flat tire, for example, or that his daughter's engagement has been broken, an Israeli might exclaim שִׂמְחָה וְשָׂשׂוֹן (*simhah ve-sason*), literally 'happiness and joy,' sarcastically, 'just my luck.'"

"Thanks for the lesson."

"By the way, חַג שָׂמֵחַ (*hag same'ah*), 'Happy holiday.'"

"*Gut yontiff.*"

96

שָׂפָה

SIN, FEH, HEH

LOOSE LIPS MAKE LANGUAGE

The Hebrew noun לָשׁוֹן (*lashon*), like the English noun for language, is derived from the word for tongue. But Hebrew is perhaps unique in that language is named for a second speech organ as well—the lips. Language in Hebrew is not only לָשׁוֹן (*lashon*), "tongue," but also שָׂפָה (*safah*), "lip."

A curious fact of Hebrew is that the plural of words for parts of the body that come in pairs—eyes, ears, lips, hands, feet, and so on—is formed by adding the ending יִם – (-*ayim*) to a slightly changed form of the singular. Thus, the plural of שָׂפָה (*safah*), when it means "lips," is שְׂפָתַיִם (*sefatayim*). All this is by way of introduction to the following curiosity: When Moses was told by God that he was to plead the case of the Israelites before Pharaoh, he tried to beg off by pleading to God that he was עֲרַל שְׂפָתַיִם (*aral sefatayim*), a "stammerer." (The literal sense of עֲרַל שְׂפָתַיִם [*aral sefatayim*] is "uncircumcised lips." Only a very few people understand for sure the physiological condition described by this term, and my *mohel* isn't telling.)

Other uses of the word שָׂפָה (*safah*) relate to the idea of a border, such as the rim of a cup, the hem of a robe, or the bank of a river. All Zionist songbooks contain the beautiful and touching עַל שְׂפַת יַם כִּנֶּרֶת (*al sefat yam kinneret*), which sings of the "shore of the Sea of Galilee."

Those etymologists who believe that the letter שׂ (SIN) and the letter ס (SAMEKH) are interchangeable can easily explain the meaning of שָׂפָה (*safah*) as "threshold" or "edge." Threshold is exactly the meaning of the expression סַף הַדֶּלֶת (*saf ha-delet*), the word סַף (*saf*) being as homonymous as you can get to שָׂפָה (*safah*). The Semitic source for both of these terms is probably the same as for סוֹף (*sof*), "ending" or "limit."

Come to think of it, the idea of the lips as a constraining limit is likely to be what the Torah had in mind when it urged the Israelites

---

מוֹצָא שְׂפָתֶיךָ תִּשְׁמֹר (*motsa sefatekha tishmor*), "You shall be careful of what comes out of your lips" (Deuteronomy 23:24). Sad to say, some of us have tended to neglect this ethical injunction, while we have been zealously attentive to what goes in through the lips.

For a review of the word כָּשֵׁר (*kasher*), go back to chapter 42.

97

תחת

TAV, HET, TAV

BENEATH THE BOTTOM LINE

One of the distinguishing characteristics of the ongoing conversation the Oral Law has with the Written Torah is the Rabbis' insistence on the figurative — as opposed to the literal — nature of biblical language. Take, for example, the famous legal principle of "an eye for an eye." The biblical phrase עַיִן תַּחַת עַיִן (*ayin tahat ayin*), the Talmud insists, refers figuratively to monetary compensation.

Conversely, in even the most poetic of biblical passages, the preposition תַּחַת (*tahat*) is often used concretely, as in the beautiful prophecy that the day will come when each of us will sit תַּחַת גַּפְנוֹ וְתַחַת תְּאֵנָתוֹ (*tahat gafno ve-tahat te'enato*), "beneath his vine and fig tree." Then there is Kohelet's philosophical lament that אֵין כָּל חָדָשׁ תַּחַת הַשָּׁמֶשׁ (*ein kol hadash tahat ha-shamesh*), "There is nothing new under the sun."

We all know that a Jewish wedding, always something new, takes place under a חֻפָּה (*huppah*), "wedding canopy." Outdoor weddings, held תַּחַת כִּפַּת הַשָּׁמַיִם (*tahat kippat ha-shamayim*), "under the canopy of Heaven," come in for particular praise.

An event that happens "here on earth" is said to take place עַל הָאָרֶץ מִתַּחַת (*al ha-arets mi-tahat*), "on the earth below." In colloquial speech, a reprehensible act is deemed מִתַּחַת לְכֹל בִּקֹרֶת (*mi-tahat le-kol bikoret*), literally, "beneath all criticism."

The root is found, in Israel, in the fields of geography, economics, criminology, and fashion. The landscape of Israel's גָּלִיל הַתַּחְתּוֹן (*galil ha-tahton*), "Lower Galilee," is always worth the trip, even if it affects the שׁוּרָה הַתַּחְתּוֹנָה (*shurah ha-tahtonah*), "bottom line," of your vacation budget. Just be sure, if you need to borrow money, you don't get involved with הָעוֹלָם הַתַּחְתּוֹן (*ha-olam ha-tahton*), "the underworld." You can be sure that they will rob you of, how shall we say, your תַּחְתּוֹנִים (*tahtonim*), "underwear."

As a noun, the word תַּחַת (*tahat*), "bottom," was originally a euphemism designating that portion of the anatomy on which one sits. As can be imagined, the Hebrew word soon found its way into vulgar speech. Interestingly, the Yiddish pronunciation of the word quickly gave birth to its own baby-language euphemisms in both English ("tushy") and Hebrew, תּוּסִיק (*tussik*).

The process is one of "measure for measure," or as they say figuratively, on the streets of Israel, תַּחַת תַּחַת תַּחַת (*tahat tahat tahat*). Thus do ancient values emerge renewed, when speakers of a living language play on both their lexical roots and their classical sources.

הוֹסָפוֹת

HOSAFOT

ADDENDA

98
TIME–SAVERS

Americans contemplating *aliyah* often look forward to a life of Mediterranean leisure. Unfortunately, many new *olim* quickly find themselves disabused of this dream on hearing their first authentic Israeli conversation. Why do Israelis speak so fast? Why does the Hebrew language have so many abbreviations? Why are there so many acronyms in which the initial letters of a string of words are taken together to form new words? What's their hurry?

Perhaps the predilection for abbreviation is not an Israeli trait but a Jewish trait. After all, the Talmud itself can be considered a shorthand recording of the deliberations of חַז"ל (*hazal*), a very frequently used expression formed from the initial letters of the expression חֲכָמֵינוּ זִכְרוֹנָם לִבְרָכָה (*hahameinu zikhronam livrakhah*), "Our Sages of Blessed Memory."

The Hebrew letters צה"ל (TSADI, HEH, LAMED) are an abbreviation for the צְבָא הֲגַנָּה לְיִשְׂרָאֵל (*tseva hagannah le-yisrael*), "Israel Defense Forces." Pronounced as a word, צַה"ל (*tsahal*), the accepted name for Israel's army, (in English, the IDF), can also be made into a verb, לְהִצְטַהֵל (*le-hitstahel*), "to be inducted into the army." The Israeli resort town of Nahariyyah is home to other soldiers too, those of the United Nations. In Hebrew, the UN is אוּ"ם (*um*), from the abbreviation of אֻמּוֹת מְאֻחָדוֹת (*umot me'uhadot*), "United Nations." Whenever a white Jeep with its distinctive markings passes by, Nahariyyans are quick to identify its occupants as אוּ"מְנִיקִים (*umnikim*), a term, by the way, of endearment.

Two of the most commonly used abbreviations in modern Hebrew sound like the English words "dash" and "canal." The first, דָ"שׁ (*dash*), is an abbreviation for דְּרִישַׁת שָׁלוֹם (*derishat shalom*), the idiom for "Best regards." The second, כַּנַ"ל (*ka-nal*), represents the abbreviation for a scholarly term כַּנִּזְכָּר לְעֵיל (*ka-nizkar le-el*), "as mentioned above," which somehow made it into everyday speech.

In Israel, abbreviations seem to be a mark of civilization. The new *oleh*, like the tourist, might be able to eat without abbreviations, but if he or she wants to use cutlery at the meal, it will be necessary to be able to ask for סַכּוּ"ם (*sakum*), a place setting made up a סַכִּין (*sakin*), "knife," a כַּף (*kaf*), "spoon," and a מַזְלֵג (*mazleg*), "fork."

Once these tools of civilization are in hand, one can proceed to masticate at a leisurely pace and contemplate the gentle Mediterranean indolence for which one came to Israel in the first place.

99
TIME-SAVERS, REVISITED

Not so long ago, there was a pedestrian safety campaign going on in Israel, whose slogan was מִלָּה שֶׁל זָהָ״ב (*millah shel zahav*), literally, "a golden word." If you look closely, however, you'll notice between the ה (HEH) and the ב (VET) of the word זָהָ״ב (*zahav*) a diacritical mark that does not normally belong there. This indicates an abbreviation and, in this case, an acronym: זָהָ״ב (*zahav*) is not only gold but a shorthand way of saying זְהִירוּת בַּדְּרָכִים (*zehirut ba-derakhim*), "caution on the roads." During this campaign, Israeli volunteers would politely ask their compatriots to cross at the רַמְזוֹר (*ramzor*), "traffic light," a combination of the words רֶמֶז (*remez*), "signal," and אוֹר (*or*), "light."

Israelis may not be famous for politeness, but they are known to love abbreviations and acronyms, and they coin them at every opportunity. At the annual Israeli book fair held in June, you can hear people asking for a מוֹ״ל (*mol*). They're not necessarily interested in an underground personality from either the spy or the animal world; rather, they're asking for directions to the stand of a particular מוֹצִיא לָאוֹר (*motsi la-or*), literally "bringer to light," idiomatically, "publisher."

The executive director of any large organization does a good deal of traveling. In Israel, to save time, you'll hear that the מַנְכָּ״ל (*mankal*) is planning a trip to חו״ל (*hul*). That's shorthand for "the מְנַהֵל כְּלָלִי (*menahel kelali*), 'director general,' will be going חוּץ לָאָרֶץ (*huts la-arets*), literally, 'out of the land,'" idiomatically again, "abroad." On returning home, the מַנְכָּ״ל (*mankal*) will be expected to present a דו״ח (*doh*), "report," from the Hebrew idiom דִּין וְחֶשְׁבּוֹן (*din ve-heshbon*), literally, "a judgment and an accounting." He or she will also be able to submit a bill for אֵשֶׁל (*eshel*), in the Bible, a "tamarisk tree." According to Rashi, the Bible commentator par excellence, this word stands for אֲכִילָה (*akhilah*), "eating," שְׁתִיָּה (*shetiyah*), "drinking," and לִינָה (*linah*), "lodging," in other words, an "expense account."

In the business world, the two abbreviations heard most frequently are בַּ״ם (*ba'am*) and מַע״ם (*ma'am*). The former applies to incorporated companies that are בְּעֵרָבוֹן מֻגְבָּל (*be-eravon mugbal*), "of limited liability." The latter term, מַע״ם (*ma'am*), is the Israeli equivalent of the Value Added Tax (V.A.T.), which in Hebrew is literally translated as מַס עֶרֶךְ מוּסָף (*mas erekh musaf*).

On your next trip to Israel, don't forget to ask – politely, of course – for the rebate on the מַע"ם (*ma'am*) that is given to tourists taking their purchases out of the country. Let's not forget that in English the word "rebate" is in its way a מִלָּה שֶׁל זָהָב (*millah shel zahav*), without the diacritical marks.

100

BASIC ARABIC

An Israeli doctor, lecturing a group of recently immigrated health-care workers, came to the problem of language: "To practice medicine in Israel," he announced, "you need to know a little bit about pathophysiology, something about symptomology, a smidgen of pharmacology ... and seventeen languages." By common consensus — and by common sense — the two most important languages of the doctor's seventeen are Arabic and Yiddish — and not only in the hospital.

Arabic is used by Israelis in situations where ardor and sharp distinctions are called for. The term יָה (*yah*) is an exclamation for surprise or enthusiasm. It is used with the Arabic term for the Deity in יָה־אָלְלָה (*yah allah*) or in the idiom יָה־בַּא־יֶה (*yah ba yeh*) to express something on the order of "Holy Cow!" יָה־אָלְלָה (*yah allah*) is also found frequently in situations that require a "Let's go!"

Arabic is used in the streets to express extreme anger. "Profanity" is a polite description of these words. Some expressions are so strong that Dan Ben Amotz and Netiva Ben Yehuda's dictionary of Hebrew slang, מִלּוֹן עוֹלָמִי לְעִבְרִית מְדוּבֶּרֶת (*millon olami le-ivrit meduberet*), *World Dictionary of Spoken Hebrew* — otherwise so graphic — shirks from giving a translation. We will follow their example here. A case in point nevertheless is an expletive referring disparagingly to the mother of one's interlocutor. Most Israelis are ignorant of the meaning of this Arabic locution, which they use frequently, in the most trivial of situations. In polite company, it is replaced by the euphemism כּוּסְאָמֶת (*kusemet*).

One of the more pleasant ways Arabic is used is in situations involving hospitality and in salutations. Everyone in Israel has at one time or another been called חֲבִּיבִּי (*habibi*) or יָה־חֲבִּיבִּי (*yah habibi*), which is different from but related to the Hebrew adjective חֲבִיבִי (*havivi*). The latter term means "my beloved"; the former, more casual, means the same thing as the French *mon vieux*, "old pal."

Walk into someone's home with an Israeli and the first word you're likely to hear from your companion is אַהֲלָן (*ahalan*), "Hi, what's new?" The host's response, in typical oriental fashion, is to double the greeting, אַהֲלָן־וַסַהְלָן (*ahalan wa-sahalan*), "Welcome, *barukh ha-ba*."

Inquire about your friend's well-being by asking כַּיפ-חָלַךְ (*kif ha-lak*), and you will elicit responses ranging from חַמְדוּלְלָה (*hamdullah*), "Thank God," to מַבְּסוּט (*mabsut*), "Okay."

When an Israeli is impatient with something, the last word out of his mouth is חַלַס (*halas*, accent on first syllable), "Enough already." The sample of Arabic given here is definitely *not* enough, but it will make conversations overheard on the streets of Israel easier to understand, or so we hope, אִנְשַׁאלְלָה (*inshalla*), "God willing."

101

BASIC YIDDISH

In what already must seem to many of us a piece of ancient history, the late Israeli prime minister Menahem Begin used to refer to Yasser Arafat as a שְׁוִיצֶר (*shvitser*). Most of us recognize the Yiddish source of this word, related to steam baths and sweating. In Hebrew, as often happens, the Yiddish meaning is shunted aside in favor of an even more colorful one. What Begin meant was to dismiss Arafat out of hand as a swaggering braggart, a *poseur*.

This derailing of meaning is common enough in Yiddish words used in Hebrew. The word גֶשֶׁפְט (*gesheft*), for example, meaning "business," is used in Hebrew to describe a business transaction that skirts the law, especially in the plural גֶשֶׁפְטִים (*gesheftim*), the ending ים- (*-im*) showing that a specifically Hebrew meaning is intended. The Hebrew word for flat tire comes from the English word for puncture, פַּנְצֶ'ר (*pantsher*). A פַּנְצֶ'ר־מָכֶר (*pantsher makher*), however, is someone who fixes flats. If a literal translation were possible, it would mean its opposite, a "puncture maker."

As with Arabic, Yiddish is used in expressions that call for profanity on the one hand, and in expressions denigrating one's fellowman on the other. These terms – borrowed from languages that are both foreign and "family" – serve as a psychological safety valve and permit the expression of anger.

A benign form of denigration is found in the word צוֹונְצִיק (*tsvontsik*), "twenty," used to describe something old, from the 1920s. (Ironic, isn't it, that a people with a five-thousand-year history, and still going strong, would consider something from a period a mere seventy-five years distant "old.") What does it mean when an Israeli portrays someone as a צַצְקֶה (*tsatske*), "toy"? It means that he's dealing with a "sharpy," someone to be wary of, a קוּנְצְמָכֶר (*kuntsmakher*), a "sharp one."

One of the more charming uses of the Yiddish language in Israel is suffused with gentle irony. When a Sephardi wishes to refer to an Ashkenazi, he calls him a ווּס־ווּס (*vus-vus*), from the Yiddish word for the question "What?" It is probably the only word in a long utterance that a nonnative speaker of Yiddish can distinguish. Nevertheless, a secular Israeli, even one who knows Yiddish and uses it as part of his Hebrew linguistic baggage, will sometimes call an ultrareligious Jew, one who on principle speaks Yiddish only, a װוּס־װוּס (*vus-vus*).

Jews are always telling jokes, probably because they're always telling stories and when you're telling stories, why not make them funny? In Israel when you tell a joke that falls flat, the best way to save face is to mutter בְּאִידִיש זֶה מַצְחִיק מְאֹד (*be-iddish zeh mats'hik me'od*), "In Yiddish it's very funny."

One of the oldest Israeli jokes concerns a citizen who tries to smuggle coffee into the country by passing it off as birdseed. Asked by the customs officer if birds would really eat that stuff, the citizen answers, "If they want to, they will; if not, not." In Hebrew it's very funny.

102

AROUND THE WORLD

In most cases it is easy to recognize the Hebrew names of the world's countries: אֲמֶרִיקָה (*amerikah*), רוּסְיָה (*rusyah*), אַנְגְלִיָה (*angliyah*), and אִיטַלְיָה (*italyah*) offer no problem, as can be seen from their transliterations. A good guesser – and what student of language is not a good guesser? – will also recognize such places as לִיטָא (*litta*), קַפְרִיסִין (*kafrisin*), and שְׁוֶדְיָה (*shvedyah*), as Lithuania, Cyprus, and Sweden, respectively.

The greatest difficulties arise where Hebrew tries to be "scientific," by tying a modern locale to biblical geography. How צָרְפַת (*tsorfat*), originally a city between Tyre and Sidon in ancient Phoenicia, became France has been shrouded in mystery for centuries and will remain so here. סְפָרַד (*sefarad*) is mentioned in the same verse in the Book of Obdiah as צָרְפַת (*tsorfat*). The use of סְפָרַד (*sefarad*) for modern Spain is a bit easier to trace. Spain, lying as it does at the westernmost edge of the Mediterranean Sea, was considered by the ancients to be where the sun goes after making its daily tour of the heavens. Vespers is the evening prayer; Hesperia, surely a cognate, is the name given to Spain by Roman poets, from "Hesperides," the mythical garden of the golden apples lying in the west. "Hesperide" in unvocalized Hebrew is הספרד. Drop the letter ה (HEH), which in Hebrew is often only a definite fiarticle, add vocalization, and you get סְפָרַד (*sefarad*). *Voilà*, as they say in צָרְפַת (*tsorfat*).

Until the dissolution of the Soviet Union, the two superpowers had a Hebrew word in common, בְּרִית (*berit*), the Hebrew term for the quintessentially Jewish notion of covenant. The Soviet Union was called the בְּרִית הַמּוֹעֵצוֹת (*berit ha-mo'atsot*), literally the "Covenant of the Councils." The Hebrew term for the United States is, of course, אַרְצוֹת הַבְּרִית (*artsot ha-berit*), literally "Lands of the Covenant."

Another of the more interesting names of today's countries is the name for China, סִין (*sin*). This does not come from the Wilderness of Sin mentioned in the Book of Exodus but from a phrase in Isaiah 49:12. When Isaiah talks of a people from an unknown land, he refers to them as a people from אֶרֶץ סִינִים (*erets sinim*).

And אֶרֶץ יִשְׂרָאֵל (*erets yisrael*), where does it come from? It derives in the first instance from the biblical story of Jacob's wrestling bout with the angel, narrated in Genesis 32:25–30. After the successful conclusion of his struggle, Jacob is told that henceforth his name will be called יִשְׂרָאֵל (*yisrael*), and then a "blessing," in the form of an etymology, is pronounced: כִּי שָׂרִיתָ עִם אֱלֹקִים וְעִם אֲנָשִׁים וַתּוּכָל (*ki sarita im elokim ve-im anashim va-tukhal*), "for you have striven with God and men and prevailed." Interestingly, from then on Jacob is still called יַעֲקֹב (*ya'akov*). His new name is subsequently given to the Land of Israel. And the people on the Land have been struggling with God and men ever since.

103
TERRIBLY TERRIFIC

A language is a mirror of a people's culture. Look into the language, and you will see reflected therein the image a people has of itself and that it projects to the world.

Modern-day Hebrew has a good deal to tell us about the quality of life in Israel. To insiders who know the lingo, life is not only טוֹב (*tov*), "good," or טוֹב מְאֹד (*tov me'od*), "very good," but מְצֻיָּן (*metsuyan*), "excellent."

Sometimes Israelis will vie with one another to proclaim the excellence of their experiences. If your neighbor heard a concert last evening that was מְצֻיָּן (*metsuyan*), then you retort that the performance you attended was מְעֻלָּה (*me'ulleh*), "superior," or even מַבְרִיק (*mavrik*), "glowing," from the same root that gives us the word בָּרָק (*barak*), "lightning." Note also how the word מְעֻלָּה (*me'ulleh*) contains within it the preposition עַל (*al*), "on top of," "above."

If your neighbor tells you that her obstetrician is יוֹצֵא מִן הַכְּלָל (*yotse min ha-kelal*), "out of the ordinary," you retort that your physician is יוֹצֵא דֹפֶן (*yotse dofen*), "extraordinary." The history of this last expression is particularly מְרַתֵּק (*meratek*), "fascinating." It seems that the word דֹפֶן (*dofen*) means "wall" and is used to connote the wall of the uterus. A fetus extracted by Caesarean section, literally "coming out through the wall," is more יוֹצֵא דֹפֶן (*yotse dofen*) than even the best obstetrician.

Hebrew slang is particularly rich in "excellence," much of it originating in the Israeli army. An Israeli soldier was recently heard to exclaim to her companion, as they both looked out at the beautiful vista afforded by the טַיֶּלֶת (*tayyelet*), "esplanade," near Talpiyot in Jerusalem, זֶה מַגְנִיב, לֹא? (*zeh magniv, lo?*), "It's breathtaking, isn't it?" Subtle readers will notice the word גַּנָּב (*gannav*), "thief," at the root of the word מַגְנִיב (*magniv*), as in, "It steals your breath away." Even more subtle readers will notice the aural consonance between the Hebrew expression זֶה מַגְנִיב, לֹא? (*zeh magniv, lo?*) and the French expression "C'est magnifique, non?"

Israeli slang is not always so subtle. Your daughter gets accepted to medical school? שִׁגָּעוֹן (*shiga'on*), literally, "madness," figuratively,

"That's great." Your daughter gets only a 78 percent on her bio quiz? Just tell her, the way an Israeli parent would, "To me, you're מֵאָה אָחוּז (me'ah ahuz), one hundred percent." And your grandchild is, of course, נֶהְדָּר (nehedar), "precious."

Was this chapter important? Some would say that is was נוֹרָא חָשׁוּב (nora hashuv), "terribly important." In this case, of course, "terrible" is a synonym for "excellent." Talk about a positive linguistic self-image.

104

CROWNS OF GLORY

Languages are logical, they say. The development of a language, on the other hand, often defies logic. How else can we account for the existence of four Hebrew words for "crown" in a culture that, to say the least, is wary of kingship?

Each of these four has developed in its own way. (For a discussion of כְּלִיל [*kelil*], see chapter 38.)

The least common word for crown is נֵזֶר (*nezer*). Students of Judaism will immediately perceive hidden in the root נזר (NUN, ZAYIN, RESH) the makings of the word נָזִיר (*nazir*), "Nazirite," one who abstains from intoxication, sex, and haircuts. Are we to conclude that a Nazirite could braid his long hair into a tiara, and that a man sporting such a נֵזֶר (*nezer*) on his head was therefore a נָזִיר (*nazir*)?

A second term for crown is עֲטָרָה (*atarah*), from the verb עָטַר (*atar*), "He encircled." The עֲטָרָה (*atarah*) was the crown given to King David. In the Torah, the word is often found coupled with a word for beauty, as in the metaphorical expression עֲטֶרֶת תִּפְאֶרֶת (*ateret tiferet*), "crown of splendor." Obviously, a crown is an adornment of great significance. For example, the famous expression עֲטֶרֶת זְקֵנִים בְּנֵי בָנִים (*ateret zekenim benei banim*), "The crown of the elderly is their children's children."

עֲטָרָה (*atarah*) is not only a crown. It is more and more frequently a name given by proud parents to their daughter. The word also designates an adornment — made of sterling silver or sometimes hand-embroidered — found on the edges of טַלִּיתוֹת (*tallitot*), "prayer shawls." Then there are those who would argue that the most culturally significant use of the word עֲטָרָה (*atarah*) can be found on the Ben Yehuda Pedestrian Mall in Jerusalem. There, in the always-bustling Cafe Atara, you will be able to rub elbows with Israeli poets, novelists, and journalists.

Strangely, the word most associated with a crown, כֶּתֶר (*keter*), has nothing to do with either David or Solomon. It is found in Scripture only in the Book of Esther. *Pirke Avot* (Ethics of the Fathers) tells us that while there are traditionally three כְּתָרִים (*ketarim*), "crowns," in Judaism — the crowns of Torah, priesthood, and kingship — there is a fourth crown that supersedes these, the כֶּתֶר שֵׁם טוֹב (*keter shem tov*), "the crown of the good name."

In modern Israel, כֶּתֶר (*keter*) is the very good name indeed of a distinguished publishing house. If you look at the spine of one of the volumes of your *Encyclopaedia Judaica*, you will see the letters "EJ" surmounted by a crown. This logo lets you know that this important reference tool was published by the Keter Publishing Company. One of the most beautiful of the Sabbath table songs contains the verse דְּעֵה חָכְמָה לְנַפְשֶׁךָ וְהִיא כֶתֶר לְרֹאשֶׁךָ (*de'eh hokhmah le-nafshekha ve-hi kheter le-roshekha*), "Seek knowledge for your soul and it will be a crown for your head."

To see how quirkily languages develop, we need only remember a fifth Hebrew word for crown. During the British Mandate, one might speak of a קְרָאוּן (*kra'un*), "crown," a coin that was worth five shillings. That the word no longer exists is a logical development not only of language but of history as well.

105

HELLO AND GOOD-BYE

Greetings and salutations. Did you know that among the contributions of Hebrew culture to the English language is the salutation "good-bye," a shortened form of "God be with you"?

In Ruth 2:4, when Boaz goes down to the field to check on the progress of the harvest, he greets his reapers with a hearty ה' עִמָּכֶם (*ha-shem immakhem*), "God be with you." In Judges 6:12, when an angel comes to Gideon to announce to the farm boy that he has been chosen to deliver Israel from the Midianites, the angel's greeting to him is ה' עִמְּךָ גִּבּוֹר הֶחָיִל (*ha-shem imkha gibbor he-hayil*), "God be with you, man of valor." (It is certainly no coincidence that the epithet גִּבּוֹר חַיִל [*gibbor hayil*], "man of valor," is also applied to Boaz.) In English, the transition among down-home folks from "God be with you" to "Good be w'ye" to "Good-bye" is easy enough to trace.

That "good-bye," which originally meant "hello," became a salutation for leave-taking is not difficult for people who use שָׁלוֹם (*shalom*) as both "hello" and "good-bye" to acccept. Nowadays, שָׁלוֹם עֲלֵיכֶם (*shalom aleikhem*), "Peace be unto you," or, more simply, שָׁלוֹם (*shalom*), "Peace," is the quintessential Hebrew greeting. Why peace? Peace is such a fundamental value in Jewish culture that the capital city of the Jews, Jerusalem, is named for peace. According to a midrash, יְרוּשָׁלֵם (*yerushalem*, note the spelling) means "foundation of peace." Do you remember the report in 1 Chronicles that King David was denied the privilege of building the Holy Temple because he was too much a man of war? That honor was to go to his son שְׁלֹמֹה (*shelomoh*), Solomon, a man of peace who had the root for peace שלם (SHIN, LAMED, MEM) in his very name.

The forms of greeting in Hebrew culture are highly ritualized. For example, שָׁלוֹם עֲלֵיכֶם (*shalom aleikhem*) is answered by עֲלֵיכֶם שָׁלוֹם (*aleikhem shalom*). The response to בָּרוּךְ הַבָּא (*barukh ha-ba*), "Welcome," is the stylized expression בָּרוּךְ הַנִּמְצָא (*barukh ha-nimtsa*), "Blessed is the one already present."

Hebrew greetings are often abbreviated. At the beginning of a business letter, you are likely to find simply א.נ. (ALEF. NUN.) or ג.נ.

(GIMMEL. NUN.). These stand for אָדוֹן נִכְבָּד (*adon nikhbad*), "Dear Sir," or גְּבֶרֶת נִכְבָּדָה (*geveret nikhbadah*), "Dear Madam," respectively.

An expression heard frequently at moments of leave-taking is ד"ש (pronounced *dosh*, rhymes with *nosh*). This is the abbreviation for דְּרִישַׁת שָׁלוֹם (*derishat shalom*). דַּ"ש לְאִמָּא (*dash le-imma*) means "Regards to your mom," or, literally, "Ask your mother for me if it is peaceful with her." To say "How are you?" in Hebrew, you ask the state of one's peace: מַה שְׁלוֹמְךָ (*mah shelomkha*, masculine) or מַה שְׁלוֹמֵךְ (*mah shelomekh*, feminine).

One of the many formal ways of ending a letter is to write בִּבְרָכָה (*bivrakhah*), "With a blessing." To אַנְשֵׁי שְׁלוֹמֵינוּ (*anshei shelomeinu*), literally, "the people of our peace," this book's family of readers, goes our בְּרָכָה (*berakhah*), for שָׁלוֹם עָלֵינוּ (*shalom aleinu*), "Peace upon us all."

Suggestions for Further Reading

This book has been designed to arouse in the reader an interest in the further pursuit of its subject matter. If, as often happens, one word leads to another, why should one book not lead to another? Readers of English will find a good deal to contemplate in the following: Philip Birnbaum, *Encyclopedia of Jewish Concepts* (New York: Hebrew Publishing Company, 1979); Lewis Glinert, *The Joys of Hebrew* (New York: Oxford University Press, 1992); Simon Glustrom, *The Language of Judaism* (Northvale, NJ: Jason Aronson, 1988, reprint); and Edward Horowitz, *How the Hebrew Language Grew* (New York: Ktav Publishing House, 1960).

Readers of *Hebrewspeak* who are also readers of Hebrew will delight in the treasures available to them. In 1975, a book of comic pieces, *Hebrew with Kishon*, by Israel's national humorist Ephraim Kishon, was published by the Hebrew Publishing Company. If you can get hold of a copy, you're in for some sidesplitting satire as well as a few well-designed vocabulary lessons and grammatical exercises. Two books available in Israel were put together from the radio and television programs of Israel's national language *maven*, Avshalom Kor. Every insightful chapter of *Yofi shel Ivrit* (Tel Aviv: Sifriyat Ma'ariv / Misrad ha-bitahon, 1986) and *Higiya Zeman Lashon* (Tel Aviv: Kinneret Publishing Company, 1994) contains a surprising yet authoritative twist about a word or idea with which you thought you were familiar. For those who are not squeamish about slang (and some vulgarity), the two volumes of *Millon Olami le-Ivrit Medubberet* (Tel Aviv: Zmora-Bitan Publishers, 1982), by Dan Ben Amotz and Netiva Ben Yehuda, provide a lively and amusing introduction to the language spoken in the streets of Israel.

To paraphrase the King Solomon of the Book of Ecclesiastes, of the buying of books about Hebrew there would appear to be no end. Since both this book and the shopping list that accompanies it here have to come to a conclusion, let it end with a recommendation for a volume that no lover of Hebrew etymology should be without, Ernest Klein's *Comprehensive Etymological Dictionary of the Hebrew Language for Readers of English* (New York: Macmillan, 1987). In more ways than one, it leads us to the last word in *Hebrewspeak*.

About the Author

Joseph Lowin is director of Cultural Services at the National Foundation for Jewish Culture. Previously, he was dirctor of the Midrasha Institute of Jewish Studies and national director of Jewish Education at Hadassah. Lowin has a Ph.D. in French language and literature from Yale University and has held faculty appointments at Yale, the University of Miami, Touro College, and Yeshiva University. He has been a Fulbright Fellow at the Sorbonne in Paris and a Jerusalem Fellow at the Hebrew University. Lowin's book *Cynthia Ozick* appeared in Twayne's United States Authors series in 1988. He has also published more than fifty articles and reviews on Jewish fiction. These have appeared in the *Jewish Book Annual*, the *Revue des Études Juives*, *Jewish Quarterly*, *Religious Studies Review*, and *Hadassah Magazine*. He is currently at work on a book about Elie Wiesel for Twayne. Joseph Lowin resides in Rockland County, New York, with his wife, Judith, and their three children.